Foreword

THE
FATHER
HEART

OF
GOD

FLOYD McCLUNG

With an update from Sally McClung

DAVID C COOK

transforming lives together

THE FATHER HEART OF GOD
Published by David C Cook
4050 Lee Vance Drive
Colorado Springs, CO 80918 U.S.A.

Integrity Music Limited, a Division of David C Cook
Brighton, East Sussex BN1 2RE, England

The graphic circle C logo is a registered trademark of David C Cook.

The website addresses recommended throughout this book
are offered as a resource to you. These websites are not
intended in any way to be or imply an endorsement on the
part of David C Cook, nor do we vouch for their content.

ISBN 978-0-8307-8480-6
eISBN 978-0-8307-8481-3

Cover Design: Pete Barnsley (CreativeHoot.com)

Printed in the United Kingdom
Revised Edition 2022

1 2 3 4 5 6 7 8 9 10

011422

CONTENTS

To my Father
Floyd McClung, Sr
who not only gave me his name
but also gave me a wonderful
example of a godly
father

FOREWORD

This is a life-changing message. Literally.

The first time *The Father Heart of God* changed my life, I was a teenager struggling to make sense of faith and life and pretty much everything in between. Somehow, Floyd McClung described the wounds in my heart and the love in the Father's heart in ways I'd never heard before. But it was his diagnosis of 'The Saul Syndrome' in chapter 8 that provoked me to pray one of the most dangerous prayers of my life.

Challenged to the core and with a shaking hand, I wrote out my own covenant with God, just like the one described here in chapter 8. Next, I climbed the hill behind my house, knelt down beside a bench and solemnly signed that piece of paper. I was inviting God to do whatever it took, no matter how long it took, to heal my heart, refine my character and release me into my fullest destiny.

I guess God heard that prayer because almost immediately everything went wrong! Suddenly I found myself in a very dark place, and this propelled me to the other side of the world. In Hong Kong, amongst addicts and scary gangsters and even scarier missionaries, the Father began healing my inner world, setting me on the path I've sought to follow ever since.

I warn you: *don't pray these prayers lightly!*

Having been impacted by Floyd McClung's message in my teens, it happened again in my late twenties. The 24-7 Prayer movement was mysteriously spreading around the world. People I'd never met were contacting me from countries I'd never heard of asking for help with things I'd never done. I was completely out of my depth.

And so, having read a few of Floyd's books over intervening years, I gathered up my courage and wrote to the great man with the funny name, requesting a little fatherly counsel. Would he, I wondered, be willing to have coffee with me, if I flew out from London to see him in Kansas City? He said it sounded like a very expensive coffee, particularly as he was imminently coming to England. Perhaps we should meet there instead?

It was to be one of the most dramatic meetings of my life. (I describe what happened in *Dirty Glory*, if you want to find out more.) As a result, Floyd became a trusted mentor to me and a champion to the 24-7 Prayer movement. Sammy and I even relocated with our two tiny sons to spend a year with him in Kansas City. Somehow, the man whose message about the father heart of God that had changed me in my teens had now become a father in God to me in my early thirties.

Of course my story about the way this book impacted my life is just one of many. Since it was first published way back in 1985, *The Father Heart of God* has never been out of print, selling more than a million copies and having been translated into 32 languages. Countless lives have been challenged, healed and changed by the simple message of this timeless classic.

Sadly, Floyd died in 2021 and I had the privilege of sharing a few words at his memorial service. Married for 54 years to Sally, he was truly a global statesman in the body of Christ. Floyd McClung led the international missions agency Youth With A Mission (YWAM) for eight years, wrote 18 books, travelled to more than 190 countries, spoke on more than 100 university campuses, and mobilised more than 400 workers in 42 nations to plant churches through his organisation All Nations. At a time when so many leaders are failing so spectacularly, it did my heart good to celebrate the life of a hero who ran the race faithfully and fruitfully, right to the very end.

Looking back, I realise that in many ways the message of this book became the message of Floyd's whole life: that the Father loves us and heals us with relentless and unconditional love, and that he sends us out to love and heal the world in just the same way.

There's something I wrote out in my journal more than 30 years ago when I first read this book, which has travelled with me ever since. Perhaps it's an appropriate note on which to conclude this foreword, introducing you with a mixture of trepidation and excitement to a message that might just be about to change your life the way it has certainly changed mine:

God is constantly thinking an uninterrupted stream of loving thoughts towards you as though nobody else in the world exists. You say, 'How does he do that? How can he be personally involved with billions of individuals at the

same time?' I don't know, but I know it's no problem for
the Creator of the world. Who knows how he does it? Just
enjoy it! (page 32)

Pete Greig
Founder of 24-7 Prayer International
Senior Pastor of Emmaus Road churches, UK

A Biography and Update from Sally McClung

Floyd McClung led a remarkable life as a global missions leader, bestselling author of 18 books, and international public speaker.

Floyd joined Youth With A Mission on missions trips during school breaks from college. He and I first met on a 1965 spring break outreach in Las Vegas, Nevada, and later married in 1967. We celebrated our honeymoon by leading a missions trip to the Caribbean.

As a young couple, Floyd and I traveled the world with YWAM and spent time at Francis Schaeffer's L'Abri Fellowship in Switzerland, which had a profound and lasting impact on our approach to community and hospitality. In 1971, we started the Dilaram House ministry in Kabul, Afghanistan, reaching out to backpackers traveling the hippie trail. Dilaram eventually expanded to a dozen countries on five continents.

In 1973, Floyd and I moved to the Netherlands to lead the work on the Ark, two houseboats moored behind Amsterdam's Central Station, where we ministered to hippies and drug addicts. Under Floyd's leadership, the Ark gained a reputation as a place of welcome, and where people could openly discuss intellectual questions about Christianity. "People don't care how much you know—until they know how much you care" was one of Floyd's favorite sayings.

After the Ark, Floyd pioneered other ministries in the Netherlands, most famously in Amsterdam's Red Light District. Situated between a Satanist church and a 24-hour adult cinema, the Cleft served as a community outreach center to the tens of thousands of prostitutes, pimps, and drug addicts who populated the area. With a heart for urban ministry, Floyd recruited young people from around the world to serve in the city, and YWAM Amsterdam eventually grew to over 300 staff and volunteers.

While living in Amsterdam, Floyd served as YWAM's International Executive Director. After 18 years in the Netherlands, we moved to California in 1991 and started the first of many leadership training and mentoring programs. In 1992, Floyd resigned from his international role in YWAM, and the following year we moved to Colorado, where we founded All Nations, an international leadership training and church planting network. Initially under the umbrella of YWAM, All Nations eventually became an independent organization, and now has hundreds of workers in over 40 countries.

Having developed a deep love of South Africa and its people during dozens of visits over a period of nearly 30 years, in 2006, Floyd fulfilled a lifelong dream, moving to Cape Town to pioneer a new All Nations ministry location. For the next 10 years, he trained and mentored young leaders, while continuing to write and travel for public speaking.

In February 2016, McClung became suddenly ill. In his final public speaking appearance, he concluded by asking a group of students, "If I can't continue, will you finish the race?" He was hospitalized within hours and never recovered.

After an extended illness, Floyd McClung went to be with his beloved Jesus on May 29, 2021, at the age of 75.

In his more than 50 years in full-time ministry, McClung spoke and lectured on over 100 college and university campuses, traveled to more than 190 countries, made dozens of TV appearances, and saw his life and work featured in countless media outlets, including Time magazine, the New York Times, CBS News, and the BBC. He founded the network of Dilaram communal houses, the 30 Days of Prayer for the Muslim World movement, and All Nations International; led Youth With A Mission for eight years; served with Billy Graham's Lausanne Movement; lived in Africa, Asia, Europe, and North America; and worked on every continent except Antarctica.

With his heart for urban missions and unreached peoples, his passion for leadership training and church planting, and his dedication to bringing the gospel to marginalized peoples—"the least, the last, and the lost"—Floyd's life impacted countless others. Loren and Darlene Cunningham, co-founders of Youth With A Mission, said of him, "Only eternity will reveal the depth and breadth of his legacy."

GRATEFUL ACKNOWLEDGEMENTS

I am very grateful for the help and advice of many friends who made it possible for me to write this book.

I am particularly grateful to my wife Sally for her love and encouragement, to my children Misha and Matthew, who were very patient with their father while I spent many hours working on this book, and to my secretary, Lura Garrido, for typing and retyping the manuscript.

Special thanks also to Linda Patton and Terry Tootle who helped Lura with the typing, and to Tom Hallas, Roger Forster, Dr Phil Blakely and Alv Magnus for the suggestions they made. Thanks to Christine Alexander and Ed Sherman for their research assistance. And I am very grateful to Dr Phil Blakely and Dr H. Wayne Light for their suggestions and help in drawing up the guidelines contained in Appendix A.

Many friends encouraged me along the way when I doubted the value of the book or my ability to finish it. I am especially grateful to Henk Rothuizen, Jon Petersen, Arne Wilkening, Wilbert van Laake, John Goodfellow, Lynn Green and John Kennedy for their timely encouragement and counsel.

I am also indebted to Mike Saia and John Dawson for the material in Chapter 2 of the book, and to Last Days

Ministries for giving permission to use portions of the tract *The Father Heart of God,* written by John Dawson (visit www.lastdaysministries.org for more information).

Most of all I am grateful to the Lord—all that is good is from him and all that is not is from me!

PREFACE

As my two children, Misha and Matthew, and I looked at the painting we experienced a feeling of great sadness. It was on a very large canvas and painted in sweeping, child-like strokes. It depicted a tall, sticklike figure with a huge square-shaped head. The dark colours and lifeless form gave it a sense of coldness and harshness. The beaklike nose and great protruding arms almost made him seem like a monster.

The title on the painting was *Man*, but according to one of the guides, in Amsterdam's Stedelijk Museum, the original title to Karel Appel's work was *My Father*.

We discussed the painting for a long time. What kind of relationship did Karel Appel have with his father? Even more important, we discussed how that affected his view of God. We wondered if Karel Appel believed in God and if so, did he believe him to be a loving Father?

I have written this book because most people do not know God as a loving Father. They do not know him as someone to love and trust, someone who is worthy of their absolute loyalty and commitment. Everyone at one time or another, whether Christian or not, gives serious thought to the question of who God is and what he is like.

This book is written to give you another way to look at God—another way besides someone or something that is removed from our daily lives.

Some people believe in God, but think he is some kind of impersonal force or a remote being that cannot be known personally.

Others want to know him personally, but struggle to do so because they view him as a kind of grandfather figure with a long grey beard, dressed in a black suit, glaring down from heaven seeking to judge anyone who dares to smile on Sunday!

One part of this book deals with God as a Father and how that relates to those of us who struggle to believe in him or trust him, because of hurts or questions or disappointing experiences.

The other part of the book deals with how we should respond to God if he is indeed a loving Father. It is one thing to talk about God—who he is and what he is like—it is quite another to talk about our responsibility towards him if he is loving and just.

I believe God has created us to be like him—only on a smaller scale of course! He created us to love each other, to care for his creation responsibly, and to be secure and confident in who we are as people. But our selfishness and emotional hurts hold us back from being the people our Father created us to be. Can you imagine what kind of wonderful world it would be if we all lived the way we were created to live?

The fact that God cares for us, and that we can be free from our selfishness and healed from our hurts, is what has given us as a family motivation to live in Amsterdam's Red-Light district, and that is also why we lived in Afghanistan for three years. It was for people like Steve, who wandered into our home in Kabul, Afghanistan one day with a very unique story to tell ...

The Wounded
Heart of Man

It was on the fifth floor of the Olfat Hotel in Kabul, Afghanistan when I saw him for the first time. He called himself Steve, but I had the feeling that wasn't his real name. His jeans were old and bleached out, not because he had bought them that way in a trendy European boutique with the ready-made 'worn look', but because of constant wear on the 'hippie-trail'. He had travelled with a friend named Jack overland from Amsterdam on the Magic Bus, a travel service that was cheap, but made no promises of safe arrival.

Steve was evasive and withdrawn, and only dropped in occasionally during the first few weeks after we met. 'We' were Sally, my wife, myself, and a few stalwart friends running a free clinic for Western drop-outs drifting across Central Asia in search of adventure, drugs and escape from the Western societies they had come to loathe. Many had been pushed to the fringes of society by rejection and a deep sense of alienation. Nothing in their surroundings provided a sense of identity or belonging. Steve was no exception.

I'll never forget the time Steve asked me if I wanted to know the happiest day of his life. Little did I realize the shock awaiting me as I expressed my eagerness to know more about this young man who until that time had remained closed, and unwilling to talk about himself or engage in normal conversation. The locked-in pain and hostility seemed to explode in a torrent of anger: 'I'll tell you the happiest day of my life,' said Steve with a strange smile on his face. 'It was my eleventh birthday and both my parents were killed in a car accident!'

I could hardly believe what I was hearing as Steve rushed on. 'They told me every day of my life that they hated me and didn't want me. My father resented me, and my mother continually reminded me that I was an accident. They didn't plan on me coming along, and didn't want me either. I'm glad they're dead!'

We lost track of Steve soon after that. But I have thought about him many times since then.

Steve was one of many young people on the hippie-trail that we befriended in Afghanistan. Many were hurting, alienated, and seeking escape from the reality of broken relationships at home.

What Sally and I discovered there, in the early seventies, was not just a few wounded westerners running away from their problems. We had come across the tip of an iceberg. These 'world travellers' were part of a whole society of hurting people. We have invested our lives since that time helping broken, hurting people, and not just young people or runaways in trouble. We have discovered that no level of society is immune to the pain of broken relationships.

At one point in the seventies it was estimated that there were ten million American women dependent on tranquillizers. One psychologist told me that 70% of all

violent-impulse crimes are committed by children from
divorced homes or single-parent families. The average parent in Europe watches television three-and-a-half hours
each day and spends thirty seconds communicating with
his children!

No, the wounded young people Sally and I found
addicted to heroin and dying in sleazy, flea-ridden 'hotels'
in Afghanistan were not an exception. They were the
product of a generation that had sown a philosophy of pri-
vatism, materialism and hedonism. Their parents denied
God, moral absolutes, and the importance of the family.
As a result, rejection and emotional scars are *normal*. My
daughter was in a class at school with twelve other children
and she was the only one from a family where both the
mother and father were still living together.

And we cannot ignore the enormous effect that modern society has on our emotions. The dependence on
computers and technology, rapid urbanization, crime and
violence, and the threat of nuclear holocaust have affected
many individuals in a profound way.

As I have already said, Steve's story is not the exception.
If we take time to care, and to listen, people begin to trust
us enough to open up and share their hurts and fears.

One upper class young man, who came to us for counselling, described how his father had made him look on
as he beat his mother and cut her with a knife; another
girl described the humiliations and molestations she had
experienced at the hands of her father, brothers and grandfather; another young man told us how his parents gave
him to his grandparents simply because they did not want
him. He was inconvenient. His grandparents in turn sent

him to an orphanage at the age of five, where he was beaten every Sunday by the Director if he refused to go to church. Years later he became a Christian through our work in Afghanistan and then returned home to express love and forgiveness to his parents with a gift, but his mother screamed at him and would not let him enter the house. Another handsome young husband wept as he said he could not remember his lawyer father telling him that he loved him even once.

We forget all too quickly that it is the norm in our world today for people to carry emotional wounds. I used to wonder why my wife and I attracted so many needy people—what was wrong with us, I asked myself? But then I came to the conclusion that when we as Christians take time to care, to create an atmosphere of love, acceptance and forgiveness, then people will open up their lives to us.

Once Sally and I sat in a prostitute's apartment in the Red Light district of Amsterdam. We listened in amazement as Annerie (not her real name) very openly described her relationship with her pimp. She and another prostitute both supported him—he lived half the day with Annerie and the other half with the other prostitute. When Sally asked why she paid this man when she knew he was living with another woman, she said after a few moments of reflection, 'Even prostitutes need someone to laugh and cry with.'

'Why?' I ask myself. Why must a prostitute pay for friendship? What has happened to our world?

I'll never forget talking to a young girl in Cornwall, who wept and sobbed as she explained how confused she was, because her father had wanted a boy. She was given a boy's name and had tried to be a boy to please him, yet she never could please him. So she carried emotional wounds with her, all because her father rejected her for being female.

Nor will I forget the girl (raised in a 'good' home of well-to-do Christian parents) who wished she was dead because her mother kept comparing her to her dead sister, saying her sister always 'did it better' than she did. Finally in desperation she felt the only way she could get her mother to love her and be pleased with her was to be dead, because her mother always talked so lovingly about her dead sister!

Is it any wonder that many people have a distorted view of God? They see him through the grid of their own experiences, and when those experiences have been hurtful, it contributes to a wrong impression of God. Many young people react violently when you talk about God as a Father. They are spiritual orphans—hurt, lonely, confused and separated.

Projecting onto God our negative experiences, deeply affects our ability to relate to him in the right way. We don't want to hear about God or talk about him. Or, if we do want to know him, we cannot approach him with love and trust. The Bible speaks of this as a 'wounded spirit' or a 'broken spirit'. The book of Proverbs says, 'A glad heart makes a cheerful countenance, but by sorrow of heart the spirit is broken' (Prov 15:13). 'A man's spirit will endure sickness; but a broken spirit who can bear?' (Prov 18:14).

One example of someone with a broken spirit in the Bible is Michal, the daughter of King Saul. She was raised in an environment that was charged with friction and conflict. Her father was an impatient man, very insecure, and given to fits of anger and jealousy. No doubt she was deeply affected by his uncontrolled anger.

Saul's jealousy of the future King David led him to devise a plot to kill David. As enticement, he offered one of his daughters to David for killing one hundred Philistines (the enemies of Israel at that time). 'Surely,' thought Saul, 'David will be killed by the Philistines and I can be rid of him for ever!'

Much to Saul's dismay David succeeded. In fact, he did more than that: he killed two hundred Philistines! Saul gave Michal as the 'prize' to David, but David soon fled from another of Saul's fits of anger and in doing so left Michal behind in the city. Several years later David returned only to find Michal married to another man. David demanded her return, against her will and that of her new husband. In the end Michal is torn from the arms of her weeping husband and forcefully returned to David (2 Sam 3:13–16).

It seems that Michal is moved between the men in her life like a pawn in a chess game. My heart goes out to her. Given the environment in which she was raised it is under-standable why Michal reacts to David with such bitterness. Michal's bitterness towards David finally comes to a head.

> As the ark of the Lord came into the city of David, Michal the daughter of Saul looked out of the window, and saw King David leaping and danc-ing before the Lord; and she despised him in her heart ... And David returned to bless his household. But Michal the daughter of Saul came out to meet David, and said, 'How the king of Israel honoured himself today, uncovering himself today before the

eyes of his servants' maids, as one of the vulgar fellows shamelessly uncovers himself!'

And David said to Michal, 'It was before the Lord, who chose me above your father, and above all his house, to appoint me as a prince over Israel, the people of the Lord—and I will make merry before the Lord. I will make myself yet more contemptible than this, and I will be abased in your eyes; but by the maids of whom you have spoken, by them I shall be held in honour, And Michal the daughter of Saul had no child to the day of her death.

(2 Sam 6:16, 20–23)

Michal was deeply hurt. Difficult as it was for her, and is for those like her, there is only one way out of the prison of hurt: forgiveness. Impossible, you say? No, not impossible. Difficult, yes, but it can be done. Many have done it and now they are free. I know because I have talked and prayed with many who have done so.

There are many modern day versions of Michal, but they don't have to end up like her, or like Steve who was so consumed with hate that he was glad his parents were dead.

What makes the difference? The father heart of God. Only he can change us and heal us and give us wholeness. But first we need to look specifically at how we are hurt and how those hurts can block the Father's love and prevent it from healing us.

2
The Father
Heart of God

She was a shy teenager, a bit taller than some, perhaps. I was tired and the last thing I wanted to do was talk to a laughing teenage girl. I had just finished teaching a group of South African young people about God's 'father heart', and I desperately wanted to rest. But something cautioned me that I should listen carefully to what she had to say.

Her question seemed almost pointless, but then I began to wonder if she wasn't struggling to tell me something else. Maybe her question was just a way of keeping the conversation going until she could say what was really on her heart? I waited, then when she had finished I asked her if there was something more she really wanted to say. She looked relieved. She sat down beside me in the small, crowded auditorium and almost whispered in my ear, 'Can I cry on your shoulder?' 'Sure,' I said, 'but can you tell me why?'

Her eyes filled with tears as the story came out. Her father had died when she was very young. Since that time she had had nobody's shoulder to cry on, no daddy to talk to about her questions and disappointments, her achievements in school and plans in life. There was an ache in her heart. She desperately missed those big loving arms to hold her and comfort her.

She cried on my shoulder, unashamedly, in front of her friends, and then we talked to our Father in heaven. We asked him together to heal that ache and fill that missing part of her life.

And he did. I saw the same girl a few years later when I was back in South Africa. I did not recognize her at first, but when she reminded me of that special time of prayer we had together the memories came flooding back. She thanked me for our time of prayer and told how it had made all the difference. In that short time together she had experienced the father heart of God.

One of the most wonderful revelations in the Bible is that God is our Father. But what do you think of when you hear the word 'father'? Do you automatically think of protection, provision, warmth and tenderness? Or does the word 'father' paint different kinds of pictures for you? God reveals himself in the Bible as a gentle, forgiving Father, desiring to be intimately involved with each and every detail of our lives. It is not only a beautiful picture, but a true one. However, every person seems to have a different idea of what God is like, because they unconsciously tend to attach feelings and impressions that they have of their own earthly father and other authority figures to their concept of their heavenly Father. Good experiences bring us closer to knowing and understanding God, just as bad experiences create distorted pictures of our Father's love for us.

Have you ever wondered why we enter the world as helpless, inadequate persons, and then slowly grow up into physically, mentally and emotionally self-sufficient adults? Have you ever asked yourself why God didn't come up with some sort of reproduction system that would produce a physically completed person such as his original creation of Adam and Eve?

I believe God wanted us to come into this world as babies, totally dependent and helpless, because he intended the family to be a place where his love is lived out in such a way that children grow up feeling understood, loved and accepted. Because of this kind of loving, secure environment, the children will feel confident about themselves and will have the same view of themselves that God has: someone who is wanted, important, valuable and good.

But what if the ideal does not happen? What if you have been failed in some way by your parents? So many have suffered hurt and rejection by their families that it is hard for them to see God as he really is, yet understanding the character of God is essential if we are to love him.

I want to look at seven different areas of misconception concerning God and his love for us. For ease of communication, I will be referring almost exclusively to God's qualities of fatherhood. However, it is important to emphasize that the Bible says that 'in the image of God he created him, male and female he created them'. In other words, both maleness and femaleness are part of God's nature and character, and a full revelation of God's love in the family is not possible unless there is both a father and mother, because they both represent unique aspects of God's character. Where there is a single-parent family, God will help compensate for the missing love of a father or mother as we pray and ask for his help, but the norm that God intended was for there to be both a father and mother because *together* they reflect a more complete picture of who God is.

I want you to look back into your personal past and see if your relationship with God has been hindered in any way because of a failure, or absence of tender loving care, from one or both of your parents in any of the following areas.

PARENTAL AUTHORITY

Have you ever turned into the driveway of a friend's house to be greeted by the family dog? The foolish creature either cowers away from you, trembling with fear, or leaps on you with an unwanted display of affection, demonstrated with tongue, tail and dirty paws! A browbeaten puppy that cannot be induced to trust you has obviously been mistreated. An exuberant dog attempting to give you a facial massage with his tongue has obviously come from a loving home! So it is, in the way man approaches God. Our past experiences influence our response when God reaches out to us.

What causes hurts in the area of authority? Imagine a bedroom door bursting open. A small boy is slapped awake by a drunk and angry man in the middle of the night. The terrified child is beaten mercilessly by the dark, hulking shape of a man he calls Daddy. What does he feel when he hears the word 'father' years later?

A fifteen-year-old prostitute with blank, empty eyes mechanically performs through a night of degradation. She doesn't care what happens to her. She hasn't felt clean since the night she was molested by her own father. One prostitute in Amsterdam asked why she shouldn't ask men to pay her now, since her grandfather had done it for 'free'.

A wounded generation stumbles through their youthful years, only to visit the same hurts on their own children. For generation after generation it continues. Is there no one to comfort us? Who will father the children of men? Whose arms are big enough for all the lonely children of the world? Who weeps over our pains? Who will comfort us in our loneliness? Only a brokenhearted father who is rejected by the little ones he yearns to heal. Our problem is that we, like the browbeaten puppy, shrink away from the One whom we assume will be like the other authorities in our life. But he is not. He is perfect love. It was God who gave this command to parents in the New Testament: 'Don't keep on scolding and nagging your children, making them angry and resentful. Rather, bring them up with the loving discipline the Lord himself approves' (Eph 6:4 TLB).

PARENTAL FAITHFULNESS

You are God's child and even now he calls your name, but maybe deep in your heart you doubt his faithfulness. As a child you may have experienced the complete absence of a father because of death or divorce. Maybe you were 'orphaned' by the demands of your parents' career. Or is it just the childhood memory of broken promises or neglect that haunts you? Did you scream for hours as a baby, while nobody came to relieve you of your discomfort and hunger? Did you whimper behind locked doors, a small child, forgotten and alone? Do you have an inability to sense his presence with you? Is your heart soft towards God or hardened with cynicism and distrust?

You may say to me, 'But if he has loved me so much, then why haven't I felt him or seen him?' It isn't God who has failed you, but those around you. Too many times we have failed to become his voice and his hands to those who do not know him. Far too few allow themselves to be led by the broken heart of Jesus to those who need to see his love demonstrated through others. Jesus is not attracted to pleasant places, but to hurting people. He pursues us with his love from our first breath until the day we die.

Your heavenly Father was there when you first walked as a child. He was there through hurts and disappointments. He is present now at this moment. You were briefly loaned to human parents who, for a few years, were supposed to have showered you with love like his love. The love and security of a good home and family were intended by God to prepare you for his love. If our parents failed us then we must recognize that fact, forgive them, and go on to open our hearts to God's love. Your loving Father awaits, even now, with outstretched arms. What keeps you from him?

Few people know God in all his loveliness while living this brief life. Many of us are like the thief who died on the cross next to Jesus. Outwardly the thief saw a bloody, disfigured body, but soon he began to perceive the true nature of Jesus, and at the last minute, entered by faith into the family of God. We too must see past the religious and commercial distortions of Jesus, and the failures of those who have rejected us, and behold the God of love who still stands with open arms saying, 'I came that they might have life, and might have it abundantly' (Jn 10:10 NASB).

'Even when we are too weak to have any faith left, he remains faithful to us ... and he will always carry out his promises to us' (2 Tim 2:13 TLB).

Parental generosity

A few years ago a friend was in a native village in the South Pacific, watching the children play. He shared with me that these children would very seldom hear the words, 'Don't touch that! Leave it alone! Be careful!' Their homes were simple, consisting of earthen floors, thatched roofs, and mats that rolled down to serve as walls at night.

In contrast, our modern homes are stuffed with expensive and fragile furnishings and appliances that represent a minefield of potential rejection and rebuke for inquisitive toddlers. How many mothers have exploded in anger at a child who has damaged a treasured object of great expense or sentimental value? Children are constantly reminded of the importance of things—their value, and how to care for them. They seldom hear the simple words, 'I love *you*'.

A repetitious and destructive chant is working its way into the subconscious minds of our children, '*Things* are more important than *me*. *Things* are more important than *me*!' What are we to do? Abandon our homes? Obviously not. But we do need to realize that our concept of God's generosity may have been crippled by our childhood experiences and that we may need to radically alter our priorities so we can communicate God's love to our children.

The truth is that God is innately generous. Creation shows an extravagance of colour, complexity and design that goes far beyond simple functional value. A tiny white flower that glistens in the sunlight high on a ledge somewhere in the Italian Alps has meaning, even if it is never seen by a human eye. It does not have economic value, but it was created by God in the hope that one day a son of

Adam or daughter of Eve might glance at it and be blessed by its beauty.

The greatest demonstration of God's father heart seems to come with his attention to the details of our life. He longs to surprise us with those extra things, those little pleasures and treasures that only a father would know we yearn for. God is not stingy, possessive, or materialistic. *We* use people as things, but *he* uses things to bless people. People are far more valuable than things. He shows his generosity in more important ways than just through material things. He gives us that which is intangible but of far greater value: forgiveness, mercy, and love.

PARENTAL AFFECTION

Do you have any idea how attractive you are to God? One of the biggest hindrances to him is when we feel our flesh is repulsive to him. When my small son is covered with mud from the back yard, I pick him up and clean him off with the garden hose. I reject the mud, not the boy.

Yes, you have sinned. Yes, you have broken God's heart. But you are still the centre of God's affections—the apple of his eye. It is *he* who pursues *us* with a forgiving heart. We say, 'I found the Lord,' but the truth is, he found us after much searching and pursuing.

Many children, particularly boys, have had no physical display of affection from their fathers, or no real compassion when they are hurt. Because of our false concept of masculinity, we are told, 'Don't cry son, boys don't cry'. Jesus is not like that. His compassion and understanding are measureless. He feels our hurts more deeply than we do because his sensitivity to suffering is so much greater.

You have forgotten most of your pains, but God hasn't. He has perfect recall of every moment of your life. Your tears are still mingled with his at this very moment.

God was there when you experienced cruel teasing in the school playground and you walked alone avoiding the eyes of the others. When you sat in a maths class confused and dejected, he was with you. At the age of four when you got lost and wandered terrified through the crowd, it was God who turned the heart of that kind lady who helped you find your mother. 'I led them with cords of human kindness, with ties of love' (Hos 11:4 NIV).

Sometimes we don't understand what a doting Father God is. Your parents may proudly display your pictures in an album, but how does that compare with God's infinite capacity to be overjoyed with your every success? It was actually God who heard you speak your first real word. The hours you spent alone exploring new textures with baby hands, were a delight to your heavenly Father. Some of his greatest treasures are the memories of your childhood laughter. There has never been another child like you, and there never will be.

Moses once invoked a blessing on each of the tribes of Israel. To one he said that they would make their dwelling place between the shoulders of God (Deut 33:12). What a fantastic blessing! That is where *you* dwell also. Whatever you become in the eyes of men—even a person of great authority, fame or title, you will never cease to be more or less than a child in the arms of God.

PARENTAL PRESENCE

There is one attribute of God that not even the best parent can hope to imitate—that is God's ability to be with you all the time. As parents we just cannot give constant attention twenty-four hours a day. We are finite beings who cannot focus on more than one thing at a time. But God is different. Not only is he with you all the time, but he gives you his whole attention. 'Let him have all your worries and cares, for he is always thinking about you and watching everything that concerns you' (1 Pet 5:7 TLB).

God is constantly thinking an uninterrupted stream of loving thoughts towards you as though nobody else in the world exists. You say, 'How does he do that? How can he be personally involved with billions of individuals at the same time?' I don't know, but I know it's no problem for the Creator of the world. Who knows how he does it? Just enjoy it!

Your parents were often preoccupied with their activities, and sometimes showed no vital interest in the small events of your life, but God is not that way. He cares. He is a God of detail. Why does the Bible say that God has numbered the hairs of your head? Not because God is concerned with abstract mathematics. He's not a computer wanting data. This picture is trying to tell us in what sort of detail he knows us and cares about our lives.

Imagine a little boy who has worked all afternoon pounding nails into pieces of scrap wood. He finally emerges from the garage and shows a three-level battleship to Mum. He can't wait until Dad gets home. Dad is late. At 6.30 a tired, preoccupied man finally arrives. A cold dinner is waiting, and so are more repairs to do on the house. The excited boy proudly displays his handiwork to a daddy who barely looks up from his calculator. Daddy never looked, but God did. Father God always looked, always took delight in the work of your hands. He's your real Father, always will be. Don't ever resent the failings of your human parents. They are just kids that grew up and had kids. Rather rejoice in the wonderful love of your Father God.

PARENTAL ACCEPTANCE

We live in a performance-orientated society. Acceptance is always conditional—if you make the football team, if you bring home a good school report, if you look pretty, if you have money, if you win—*then* you are accepted and 'loved'. But God is a God of *unconditional* love. His love is not based on performance. He loves us because *he is love*. God's promises are conditional; we must obey him to see blessing, but his love is unconditional. This means that because he is love, by his very nature and his choices, we don't need to do anything to get him to love us. We do need to come to him and receive his love, but that does not mean we have to become a saint first. Come as you are. Just be honest with him. He delights to forgive you. Even in the depths of your past rebellion he loved you.

You may have an inability to receive God's love and approval. A true love relationship involves the giving and receiving of love. Imagine how I would feel if I was in a romantic mood one day and decided to buy my wife some flowers, and when I handed them to her and said, 'I love you, Sally,' she ran to get some money to pay for the flowers. I don't want her to do that! All I want is a response of her love in return for mine. I want to know that she feels the same way about me.

What is your response to God when he simply says he loves you? Can you receive his love without rushing into frantic activity to earn his approval? One of the greatest pictures of human peace and contentment is that of a baby asleep in the arms of his mother, after having been fed at the breast. The child no longer squirms and demands, but rests in the embrace of loving arms. A deep, mellow contentment wells up into the sound of a lullaby sung by mothers at times like this. In the Bible the prophet Zephaniah described a similar emotion in the heart of God for us: 'The Mighty One will save; he will rejoice over you with gladness, he will quiet *you* in his love, he will rejoice over you with singing' (Zeph 3:17).

God already loves you. All through life you have had to perform and compete. Even as a tiny baby you were compared with other babies. People said you were 'too fat' or 'too thin', or had 'his legs' or 'her nose'. But God delighted in your uniqueness and still does.

Yes, there is much to be done in your life and through your life. There will be days when God brings to you a deep understanding of areas of sin and selfishness in your life that need to be changed and submitted to him. But God is not always demanding changes. He knows our limits and he gives us grace and power to do the things he asks of us. He is tender and compassionate. Most of the time he just says, 'I love you'. Even when he is unhappy about the things we have done, he still loves us. My children once learned a song that beautifully summarizes God's great love for us:

> Jesus loves me when I'm good,
> When I do the things I should.
> Jesus loves me when I'm bad,
> Even though it makes him sad.

PARENTAL COMMUNICATION

Do you have difficulty looking people in the eye? Was the only time you had eye-contact with your parents when they yelled at you or criticized you?

Open, warm communication is very difficult for many parents, especially men. But God always communicates his love to us. In fact, he loves us so much 'that he gave his only begotten Son, that whosoever believeth in him should not perish, but have everlasting life' (Jn 3:16 AV).

One girl told me she couldn't pray. It seemed that heaven was a brick wall. She could not remember ever hearing God speak to her in her own heart. As we prayed together, she realized that she saw God as if he were her own father—a good man, but a man who was very quiet and shy. He rarely spoke to his children and never told them he loved them. When she admitted that her father had been weak, even failed her, she was able to forgive him and accept him as he was. This opened up a whole new dimension in her relationship with God. Faith was released in her heart to pray, knowing that God heard her. She in turn heard God speaking to her heart.

If you see that you have been hindered in your relationship with God, due to some kind of parental failure, then take these things to the Lord. You must have forgiveness in your heart towards anyone who has hurt you. If you don't, bitterness will consume you and you will find no peace with God. Realize too that you are not alone. I haven't met a perfect person yet, or a parent who hasn't made mistakes. Everyone has suffered some kind of hurt in their life. The important thing is that you get to know God for who he really is—not who you *think* he is. He is the perfect parent. He always disciplines in love. He is faithful, generous, kind and just. He loves you and he longs to spend time with you. He wants you to receive his love, and know that you are a special and unique person to him. Will you receive God's love and affection? Will you open up and enter into an intimate relationship with your true Father? He is patiently waiting for you to come to him.

3

THE WAITING FATHER

They say that the first time Sawat went to the top floor of the hotel, he was shocked. He had never dreamed it would be like this. Every room had a window facing into the hallway and in every room sat a girl. Some looked older and they were smiling and laughing, but many of them were just twelve or thirteen years old—some even younger. They looked nervous, even frightened.

It was Sawat's first venture into Bangkok's world of prostitution. It all began innocently enough, but soon he was caught up in it like a small piece of wood in a raging river. It was too powerful for him, too swift, and the current too strong.

Soon he was selling opium to customers and propositioning tourists in the hotels. He even went so low as to actually help buy and sell young girls, some of them only nine and ten years old. It was a nasty business, and he was one of the most important of the young 'business men'.

Sawat became a central figure in one of the world's largest and most loathsome trades: Thailand's sex industry. It is estimated that over 10% of all girls in Thailand end up in prostitution. The top floors of most hotels are used by them, as are the back rooms of many bars. Though the practice is discouraged by the Royal Family, many poorer rural families sell their young daughters to pay off family debts. Who knows what happens to many of these frightened ten-year-olds when they have outlived their usefulness?

Sawat disgraced his family and dishonoured his father's name. He had come to Bangkok to escape the dullness of village life. He found excitement, and while he prospered in this sordid life, he was popular. But then the bottom dropped out of his world. He hit a string of bad luck: he was robbed and while trying to climb back to the top, he was arrested. Everything went wrong. The word spread in the underworld that he was a police spy. He finally ended up living in a shanty by the city rubbish dump.

Sitting in his little shack, he thought about his family, especially his father. He remembered the parting words of his father, a simple Christian man from a small village in the south, near the Malaysian border: 'I am waiting for you.' Would his father *still* be waiting for him after all he had done to dishonour the family name? Would he receive him home after disregarding all he had been taught about God's love? Word had long ago filtered back to his village about his life of crime and sin.

Finally, he devised a plan.

'Dear Father,' he wrote, 'I want to come home, but I don't know if you will receive me after all that I have done. I have sinned greatly, Father. Please forgive me. On Saturday night I will be on the train which goes through our village. If you are still waiting for me will you tie a piece of cloth on the po tree in front of our house?'

During the train ride he thought over his life of evil. He knew his father had every right to refuse to see him. As the train finally neared the village he was filled with anxiety.

What would he do if there was no white piece of cloth on the po tree?

Sitting opposite Sawat was a kind stranger who noticed how nervous his fellow-passenger had become. Finally, Sawat could stand the pressure no longer. The story burst out in a torrent of words. He told the man everything. As they entered the village, Sawat said, 'Oh, sir, I cannot bear to look. Can you watch for me? What if my father will not receive me back home?'

Sawat buried his face between his knees. 'Do you see it sir? It's the only house with a po tree.'

'Young man, your father did not hang *one* piece of cloth … look! He has covered the whole tree with pieces of white cloth!' He could hardly believe his eyes. There was the tree, covered, and in the front yard his old father was dancing up and down, joyously waving a piece of white cloth! His father ran beside the train, and when it stopped at the little station he threw his arms around his son, embracing him with tears of joy. 'I've been waiting for you,' he exclaimed!

A man had two sons. When the younger told his father, 'I want my share of your estate now, instead of waiting until you die,' his father agreed to divide his wealth between his sons.

A few days later this younger son packed all his belongings and took a trip to a distant land, and there wasted all his money on parties and prostitutes. About the time his money was gone a great famine swept over the land, and he began to starve.

He persuaded a local farmer to hire him to feed his pigs. The boy became so hungry that even the pods he was feeding the swine looked good to him. And no one gave him anything.

When he finally came to his senses, he said to himself, 'At home even the hired men have enough and to spare, and here I am, dying of hunger! I will go home to my father and say, "Father, I have sinned against both heaven and you, and am no longer worthy of being called your son. Please take me on as a hired man".'

So he returned home to his father. And while he was still a long distance away, his father saw him coming, and was filled with loving pity and ran and embraced him and kissed him.

His son said to him, 'Father, I have sinned against heaven and you, and am not worthy of being called your son'.

But his father said to the slaves, 'Quick! Bring the finest robe in the house and put it on him. And a jewelled ring for his finger, and shoes. And kill the calf we have in the fattening pen. We must celebrate with a feast. For this son of mine was dead and has returned to life. He was lost and is found'. So the party began.

                              (Lk 15:11–24 TLB)

What a beautiful picture of God these two stories paint for us. The biblical story is often called 'The Prodigal Son', but I think it would be better titled 'The Waiting Father'. There are three aspects of the character of the father in both stories, particularly the biblical parable, that help us understand the father heart of God.

He loved his son enough to let him leave home. He had spent so long preparing his son for adulthood. In the Jewish tradition this meant many hours of teaching him the laws of God. Though he knew what kind of misfortune could befall his younger son, and though he tried to prepare him to be a righteous and responsible member of the Jewish congregation and community, he wisely allowed his son to go, without protest or pressure.

This father understood the purpose of discipline and training. More than outward obedience, he wanted to win the heart of his young son. Now that his son had reached the age where he could ask for his part of the family wealth, as Jewish tradition allowed, the father did not dissent even though it seemed callous and presumptuous of his headstrong son to demand his share of the family wealth at such a young age.

The father was creating the possibility for true relationship through his willingness to allow his son this freedom. Though inwardly he grieved over his son, he did not try to force a relationship with him. He simply made himself available to serve his son as he had always done. He did not give his son this amount of freedom because he agreed with him, but because he loved him and because he was wise enough to wait for his son to want that relationship. He had spent years instructing him in the way he should go. He had spent hundreds of hours teaching him the wisdom found in God's laws. He had been cultivating a friendship with his young son since he was born.

Now the son must choose.

And the father let him go. He knew that to force him to stay against his will was to demand outward conformity without heart relationship. He understood God enough to know that you could live by the law of Moses, and at the same time your heart could be worshipping and longing for other gods. No, he wanted a relationship with his son more than forced obedience, but he must wait until he was ready for that. He would pray and he would wait. His heart would follow his son, but he must wait for him to come back home.

For a father to respond in this way to his rebellious son shows how much this father understood the heart of God. God sovereignly chose to give man free will, and when he did that he took the risk of being rejected. God did not want 'religion'—that is, an impersonal and involuntary obedience to a set of rules. He wanted heart relationship with those whom he created. There is always a risk in giving people freedom of choice, but without that risk there is no true heart relationship. It is not that he wants people to choose against him, but any other solution than our personal freedom would be a violation of true relationship.

This kind of freedom can be violated if we do not give other people the same freedom God gives us. For us to try to force conformity, belief, or obedience, by pressure, threats, rules, withdrawing friendship, making demands or anything else, is to destroy the very heart of Christianity. It is to destroy the grace of God and enter into a religious legalism.

All too often those who are insecure tend to find their security in outward conformity to religious rules, or in the approval of people, rather than putting their security in their personal relationship with Jesus Christ because of his death on the cross.

He loved his son so deeply that he watched every day for him to return home. There is a story told about a man who came every night to a large auditorium to hear a famous evangelist preach the gospel. Night after night he came, yet he was unmoved in his firm conviction that there was no reason to go forward in response to the appeals to make a public commitment to Jesus Christ. 'I can pray right here where I'm sitting,' thought the man. And each night he returned to hear more, always sitting in the same place. Night after night a polite young usher approached the well-to-do visitor and asked him if he would like to go forward to make a public commitment to follow Jesus Christ.

And each time the man told the young usher, 'I can pray right here where I'm sitting, young man. I don't need to go forward to pray or become a Christian!' And this usher always responded courteously, 'I'm sorry, sir, but you are wrong. You cannot pray here. You must go forward if you want to make a commitment to accept Jesus Christ as your Lord and Saviour'. This conversation was repeated almost verbatim every night, but the business man was determined not to respond with a show of 'public emotion', as he called it.

But then came the last night in the series of meetings. The distinguished-looking man took the same seat he had occupied each night previously. The evangelist preached and for the last time he invited people in the audience to respond, by coming to the front of the auditorium, to indicate their desire to give their lives to Jesus Christ. Once more the usher invited the man to go to the front. 'I'll go with you, sir,' he said, 'if you want to go to the front to give your life to Christ.'

This time the man looked up with tears in his eyes. He had been deeply touched by the preaching. He replied to the young man, 'Oh, would you please go with me. I need to give my life to Christ. I'm ready to go forward and pray'. To which the usher replied, 'Sir, you don't need to go forward to accept the Lord. You can pray right here where you are sitting!'

When this distinguished man was ready to humble himself, then the Lord could respond to him where he was. The lost son finally came to the same attitude. He acknowledged his guilt. It was then that the change took place in his heart. His father was wanting him to reach this attitude of brokenness and sorrow for his sin. The father longed earnestly to have an unbroken heart relationship with his wayward son, but he knew that was not possible unless his son had a change of heart. Every day his father stood at the end of the road and watched for him. How he longed for him to return. How great was his patience and compassion.

The son could not blame his father for his problems. He ended up eating with pigs because of his own foolishness. When he realized how foolish he had been, he repented of his selfishness, and decided to return home to his waiting father. In this story, grace and repentance meet each other. Because he knew his father was so loving, the son decided to return home, acknowledging his wrong attitude and actions. It was the knowledge of his father's love that finally brought him to the place of repentance. I believe that to know the Father is to love him! And to love the Father is to return to him.

Our heavenly Father longs for us to return 'home'. Whatever your problem, whatever your need, the Father is waiting for you to return to him. The Bible says that 'the Lord waits to be gracious to you; therefore he exalts himself to show mercy to you' (Is 30:18). In another place it says, 'Do you not know that God's kindness is meant to lead you to repentance?' (Rom 2:4).

He is the waiting Father.

He loved his son so much that when he did return home he did not condemn his son for his wrong actions, but forgave him and celebrated his return with a great feast! What a great father! In fact, as we read this parable again, we notice that he is not just a waiting father! He is the running father. When he sees his dirty, weary, guilty son coming down the road, hesitant and uncertain about his father's response to him, he runs to him and puts his arms around him and embraces him. There is no reserve in his heart towards this one who has sinned. He is totally forgiving. His joy says it all.

See what manner of love the Father has given to us! He calls us 'son', or 'daughter'. We are princes and princesses. We belong to the King. He is our Father! He does not force us to be his. It is our choice and when we do rebel and act selfishly, he doesn't grow cold and hard, and ignore us. He weeps over us and waits for us. Every day he looks for us, anxiously awaiting our return. And when we come back he celebrates our return with a great, joyful banquet.

He does not condone our rebellion or selfishness. It grieves him deeply to see us hurting ourselves and others. It is wrong and we know it, for he has told us often. It is his grief, his broken heart, his compassion, his willingness to give so much love that finally wins our hearts. To know him is to love him. And to love him is to obey him.

And we should not think that because he is so forgiving his love is sentimental or soft. He is strong. He can roar like a lion. There is great strength in his quietness—no one who knows him can doubt that. He is no hollow God. His ruthless hatred of evil tolerates no double-mindedness, but his compassion is endless towards those who see their need of him. He sees our hearts. He knows our innermost thoughts. There is great security beneath the gaze of those pure, piercing eyes for all those who sincerely want to be in his family.

The Bible describes the character of our waiting Father in many ways. It leaves no room to blame him for any injustice. Though many blame him for their problems and their hurts, it is clear that his character is without blemish. Consider just some of these qualities the Bible teaches about God.

1. Creator

One who creates us in his image, with freedom to choose whether to respond to his love.

'In him we live and move and have our being ... for we are indeed his offspring' (Acts 17:28).

'Oh Lord, thou art our Father; we are the clay, and thou art our potter; we are all the work of thy hand' (Is 64:8).

2. Provider

One who loves to provide for our physical, emotional, mental and spiritual needs.

'If you then, who are evil, know how to give good gifts to your children, how much more will your Father who is in heaven give good gifts to those who ask him!' (Mt 7:11).

3. Friend and counsellor

One who longs to have intimate friendship with us and to share wise counsel and instruction with us.

'Thou art the friend of my youth' (Jer 3:4).

'And his name will be called Wonderful Counsellor, Mighty God, Everlasting Father, Prince of Peace' (Is 9:6).

'Thou dost guide me with thy counsel' (Ps 73:24).

4. Corrector

One who lovingly corrects and disciplines us.

'My son, do not regard lightly the discipline of the Lord ... for the Lord disciplines him whom he loves, and chastises every son whom he receives .... If you are left without discipline ... then you are illegitimate children and not sons. For the moment all discipline seems painful rather than pleasant; later it yields the peaceful fruit of righteousness to those who have been trained by it' (Heb 12:5– 6,8,11).

5. Redeemer

One who forgives his children's faults and brings good out of their failures and weaknesses; one who brings us back from being lost.

'The Lord is merciful and gracious, slow to anger and abounding in steadfast love. As far as the east is from the west, so far does he remove our transgressions from us. As a father pities his children, so the Lord pities those who fear him' (Ps 103:8,12–13).

6. Comforter

One who cares for us and comforts us in times of need.

'Blessed be the God and Father of our Lord Jesus Christ, the Father of mercies and God of all comfort, who comforts us in all our affliction' (2 Cor 1:3).

7. Defender and deliverer

One who loves to protect, defend and deliver his children.

'He who dwells in the shelter of the Most High, who abides in the shadow of the Almighty, will say to the Lord, "My refuge and my fortress; my God, in whom I trust". For he will deliver you ...' (Ps 91:1–3).

8. Father

One who wants to free us from all false gods so that he can be a Father to us.

'And I will be a father to you, and you shall be my sons and daughters says the Lord Almighty' (2 Cor 6:18).

9. Father of the fatherless

One who cares for the homeless and the widow.

'Father of the fatherless and protector of widows is God in his holy habitation. God gives the desolate a home to dwell in' (Ps 68:5–6).

10. Father of love

One who reveals himself to us and reconciles us to himself through Jesus Christ.

'For the Father himself loves you, because you have loved me and have believed that I came from the Father' (Jn 16:27).

There are many other terms in the Bible used to describe the character of our Father God. Listed below are a few of those terms and Scripture references you may want to refer to, as you meditate on the character of our wonderful God. He is:

Patient	Ps 78:35–39
Considerate	Jn 2:1–11; 19:25–27
Holy	Jn 2:13–22
Discerning	Jn 2:23–25
Compassionate	Lk 19:1–10
Sensitive	Lk 8:40–48
Caring	Mt 9:35–38
Tender	Jn 12:1–8
Gracious	Jn 4:7–27
Forgiving	Jn 8:1–11
Just	Deut 32:4–5
Loving and Kind	Ex 34:6–7
Merciful	Lam 3:23; Lk 23:29–43
Thoughtful	Lk 18:15–17
Generous	Mt 14:13–21; 15:30–38
Powerful	Mt 17:14–21
Wise	Mt 17:24–27
Mighty	Mk 4:35–41
Loving	Lk 6:27–36

Despite all that the Bible teaches about God as loving and just, there was a time in my life when I respected him, but I did not love him. I even feared him, because of his awesome power, but I did not love him for his goodness.

It was when I looked beyond my ideas about God, beyond my desire to argue and discuss, and asked God to reveal to me how he saw my selfishness, that I began to experience a deeper relationship with God.

It was then that I discovered the broken heart of God.

4

THE BROKEN HEART OF GOD

I had spent a long week lecturing and counselling in Norway and I was exhausted. I love being with people, but by the end of a week consisting of eighteen-hour days, I just wanted to be alone. I was 'people tired'.

As I climbed out of the taxi in front of Oslo's International Airport, I sent a silent prayer heavenward. My request was simple enough: all I wanted was a seat to myself on the aeroplane, with a little extra legroom (for my two metre frame) to spread out and rest on the three-hour flight back to Amsterdam.

Walking down the centre aisle of the plane, slightly stooped over to avoid hitting my head on the ceiling, I found an empty row of seats, by a bulkhead no less, so that meant extra legroom and a quiet flight back to Schiphol Airport. I smiled to myself smugly as I turned to sit down in the aisle seat, thinking how good God was to answer my prayer for a little rest and peace. 'God understands how tired I am,' I thought.

As I turned to take my seat, a smiling, rather dishevelled man came up the aisle and greeted me boisterously. 'Hi! You an American?'

'Yes ... yes I am,' I said with some lack of enthusiasm, as I continued to sit down. I chose the aisle seat thinking it would be harder for anyone to sit by me since they would have to step over my long legs! I heard the man who greeted me sit down in the seat behind me, but I paid him no attention as I settled down to do a little reading.

After a few minutes his head came around the corner. 'Whatcha reading?' he asked as he peered over my shoulder. 'My Bible,' I replied a bit impatiently. Couldn't he see I wanted to be alone? I settled back in my seat, but a few minutes later the same pair of eyes were again looking over the top of my seat. 'What kind of work do you do?' he asked.

Not wanting to get involved in a long conversation, I decided to make my answer brief. 'A kind of social work,' I said, hoping he wouldn't be interested. It bothered me a little that I was verging on not telling the truth, but I dared not tell him I was involved in helping needy people in the inner city of Amsterdam. That would be sure to provoke more questions.

'Mind if I sit by you?' he asked as he stepped over my crossed legs. He seemed to be oblivious to my efforts to avoid talking to him. He turned to face me and he reeked of alcohol. He spat as he spoke, sending a fine spray all over my face.

I was deeply irritated by this man's obnoxiousness. Couldn't he see I wanted to be alone? All my plans for a quiet morning were destroyed by his insensitivity. 'Oh God,' I groaned inwardly, 'please help me.' The conversation moved slowly at first. I answered a few questions about our work in Amsterdam, and began to wonder why this man wanted so desperately to talk to someone. As the conversation unfolded it dawned on me that perhaps I was the one who was being insensitive.

'My wife was like you,' he said after a while. 'She prayed with our children, sang to them and took them to church. In fact,' he said slowly, his eyes misting over, 'she was the only real friend I ever had.'

'Had?' I asked. 'Why are you referring to her in that way?'

'She's gone.' By this time the tears were beginning to trickle down his cheeks. 'She died three months ago giving birth to our fifth child. Why?' he gasped, 'Why did your caring God take my wife away? She was so good. Why not me? Why her? And now the government says I'm not fit to care for my own children, and they're gone too!'

I reached out and took his hand and we wept together. How selfish, how insensitive I had been. I had only been thinking of my need for a little rest when someone like this man desperately needed a friend. He filled in the rest of the story for me. After his wife died, a government appointed social worker recommended that the children be cared for by the state. He was so overwhelmed by grief that he couldn't work, so he also lost his job. In just a few weeks he had lost everything, his wife, his children and his work. It was December so he had decided to leave; he couldn't bear the thought of being at home alone for Christmas without his wife or children, and he was literally trying to drown his sorrows in alcohol.

He was almost too bitter to be comforted. He had grown up with four different step-fathers and he never knew his real dad. All of them were hard men. When I mentioned God he reacted bitterly. 'God?' he said. 'I think if there is a

God he must be a cruel monster! Why did your loving God do this to me?'

As I flew on the aeroplane with that wounded, hurt man, I was reminded again that many people in our world have no understanding of a loving God—a God who is a loving Father. To speak of a loving God, a God who is a Father, only evokes pain for them. And anger. To speak of the father heart of God to these people, without empathizing with their pain, verges on cruelty. The only way I could be a friend to that man, on the trip from Oslo to Amsterdam, was to *be* God's love to him. I didn't try to give pat answers. There were none. I just let him be angry and then poured some oil on his wounds. He wanted to believe in God, but deep inside his sense of justice had been violated. He needed someone to say that it was okay for him to be angry, and to tell him that God was angry too. By the time I had listened and cared and wept with him, he was ready to hear me say that God was more hurt than he was by what had happened to his wife and family.

No one had ever told him that God has a broken heart.

He listened in silence as I explained that God's creation was so marred by sin and selfishness, that it is completely different now from how he created it. It is fallen. It is not normal. The question that he asked, of course, and that all of us ask at one time or another is, why? Why does God allow it to happen? Why doesn't he intervene? Why did he create something that could become fallen and marred? If he is a loving Father, why does he allow all the suffering and injustice that goes on in our world?

I tried to help him with the answers to these questions that had helped me, but I would greatly stress that before we ever try to answer these questions with our 'head' we must feel them with our heart. It is profoundly insensitive to treat those kinds of questions merely as some kind of intellectual exercise. If we do feel deeply about suffering and are sensitive to the suffering of others, then I believe we can point in the right direction to show the answers. We must remember it is out of hurt, not just rebellion, that some people deny God's existence. When they experience suffering they lash out at God. It is incomprehensible to them that he could be good yet tolerate evil in his universe. So they deny his existence.

But lashing out at God obviously does not solve the problem. If there is no personal infinite God, *suffering loses all meaning*. If there is no God, man is just a complex product of chance, and 'suffering' is just the result of an evolutionary process, a physical-chemical problem of development. It is perhaps a case of the survival of the fittest, but if there is no God, there are no moral absolutes, and therefore no basis to say that any form of suffering is morally wrong. By denying his existence we are denying any meaning to life itself, and therefore we are saying that it really makes no difference whether people suffer or not. We could not even ask the question, 'Why do the innocent suffer?' because there is no such thing as innocence. Innocence implies guilt, and guilt implies that some things are absolutely, morally wrong.

I believe suffering is wrong, and the very fact that God does exist allows us to say that so emphatically. But that brings us to another important consideration.

How does God feel about suffering and evil in his creation? The Bible answers that question very directly. It says that it brings great sorrow to his heart.

'The Lord saw that the wickedness of man was great in the earth, and that every imagination of the thoughts of his heart was only evil continually. And the Lord was sorry that he had made man on the earth, and it grieved him to his heart' (Gen 6:5,6).

We have asked questions up to this point that deal with the justice of God. Now let's turn it around and ask questions about *our* response to evil and suffering. Do we react just as deeply as God does to evil in the world? More importantly, how do we react to evil in our own lives? Have we shared the sorrow of God's heart over sin, and what it does to bring destruction to all that it touches? It is hypocritical to say we care about suffering in the world, if we have not grieved deeply over the suffering our own selfishness has brought to God and to others.

Sin grieves God's heart. My sin and your sin has brought great sorrow to his heart. Because this is not just an intellectual exercise, and I assume you would not be reading a book like this, unless you were committed to the pursuit of truth with real integrity, may I suggest that you stop now and think about this very important question? If you have never experienced God's sorrow over sin, why don't you ask him to bring true sorrow to your heart over sin and its results?

We can never experience complete healing for our emotional wounds, or fully receive the Father's love unless we share God's sorrow over sin and selfishness. The Bible teaches that there is a difference between godly sorrow and worldly sorrow over sin. Paul wrote to the Corinthian Christians and said, 'I rejoice, not because you were grieved, but because you were grieved into repenting, for you felt a godly grief, so that you suffered no loss through us. For godly grief produces a repentance that leads to salvation and brings no regret, but worldly grief produces death (2 Corinthians 7:9–10).

Repentance is not just being sorry, it is being sorry enough to stop doing wrong. Godly sorrow is not just confessing our sins. If we confess our sins, but keep on committing them, we have not really experienced godly grief. Nor is repentance just feeling bad about what we have done. Sometimes we feel bad simply because we have been caught, or we feel bad if we have to stop sinning, but godly sorrow is not based on feeling or selfish motives. Godly sorrow is based on how sin hurts God and others. Godly sorrow produces a change in our attitude to sin itself. We begin to hate sin and love goodness.

Godly sorrow also results in a new respect for God and his laws. His laws are very reasonable when you think about them: do not kill, do not steal, do not lie, do not take other people's husbands or wives, and so on. To obey these laws is not living by an outside, imposed morality, but it is living the way we were created to live. Cars are 'created' to drive on roads—not through canals, over fields or off the sides of mountains; they were made to be powered by petrol, not water or coca-cola. Some people might say that it's no fun unless you can drive cars in lakes and off the sides of mountains, but nevertheless they were not created to be driven that way! Unless you use a car for its intended purpose you will destroy it.

So it is with us. God created us to love one another, to be kind, unselfish, forgiving, honest, loyal to our husbands and wives, and to recognize him and live in fellowship with him. Actually, the very heart and meaning of our existence is found in loving God. If we do love God, obeying his laws will come very naturally. We should not attempt to obey God's laws in order to go to heaven, or escape going to hell, or to be well respected, or get something from God. We should obey God's laws because he loves us and we want to respond to his love by pleasing him with our words and actions. Obedience is a *love response* to God!

In Amsterdam there are laws against a man beating his wife. Now, I do not beat my wife, nor do I have to have a policeman follow me around with a gun at my back, saying: 'I'm right behind you so you had better not beat your wife!' Why don't I beat my wife? Is it fear of the law that motivates me? No! It is *love*.

Sharing God's broken heart also frees us to hate what he hates, without feeling that we have lost our integrity. Many people hate God because of religion. They have associated him with all the junk and hypocrisy they have seen in Christianity, and they have rejected him as well as the junk.

Most agnostics have given up on God because of the false image of God or Christ given by the church. I think the Australians are a classic example of this. Some people, even some Australians themselves, will tell you that most Australians couldn't care less about God. But I don't believe that. They have not simply rejected God, they have rejected false images of God. The god they reject, I reject also.

When Bob Hawke became Prime Minister of Australia he gave an interview, during which he said he had learned to care about the working man from his father's deep care for the working class, which was derived from his belief in the fatherhood of God. But Bob Hawke threw out his faith in God because of a disillusioning experience with the church while attending a conference in India.

John Smith, an Australian friend, said in a University mission lecture, that there are three false images of God that Australians have rejected, thinking they have rejected the God of the Bible:

1. The God of indifference
2. The God of privilege and prosperity
3. The God of arbitrary judgement.

Early Americans went to America because of their convictions, but Australians were sent to Australia *for* their convictions. One writer suggested that sending unwanted criminals from England to Australia was like sending your sewage as far away as possible from your house! Some men were sent for as little as stealing a loaf of bread. Australia was seen as a giant penal colony. Many of the prison wardens were priests and ministers. Can you imagine how most men felt about God if they were sent unjustly to an Australian prison and their sentence was enforced by a priest or minister? As John Smith says, 'Australia has a history that causes many not to believe in God, when really they should not believe in man!'

If you have been offended by hypocrisy in the church, or if you have rejected an arbitrary God that gives men laws they cannot keep and then sends them to hell for not keeping them, or if you are angry about injustice and poverty and have been presented with a God who does not care, then you can start again without losing your integrity. You have not been rejecting the God of the Bible. You have not rejected Jesus Christ!

The God of the Bible, the God who has revealed himself in Jesus Christ, hates hypocrisy. He is angry at injustice. The difference between God and us is not anger over injustice, but the fact that he is absolutely just and we are not.

People, like the man I met on the aeroplane, get angry at God because they are hurt—either through personal disappointment or through reaction to injustice in the world around them. But a humble, honest man cannot take out his anger permanently on God because he must eventually acknowledge that he is guilty of the very things he accuses God of doing! We have all committed the same sins as the greatest criminals in history. We don't want to see ourselves that way, and of course we have not necessarily done it to the same degree, nor have we necessarily let our selfishness dominate us to the same extent, but in word or thought, and sometimes in deed, we express the same sins that we condemn in others. We condemn Hitler ruthlessly, but are we just as ruthless in dealing with hatred in our own hearts? 'I don't hate the Jews,' you may say. But is there someone you hate? One of your neighbours perhaps? Or a fellow student? Someone you work with? If we have *hated* someone, anyone, it is the very same attitude that motivated Hitler.

A proud man keeps on accusing God, because he refuses to admit his own guilt. To deal with evil in the world we must begin with ourselves. If we don't accept our own responsibility for evil we will eventually reject God's explanation for good and evil, and come up with a reason or philosophy that excuses us personally from bowing before him and acknowledging his right to rule over our lives.

If we believe in God, but still accuse him of being unjust, we have never humbled ourselves to the extent that we have been able to see how our selfishness has brought grief to his heart.

The heart of God is broken. Sin has broken his heart. My sin and your sin, and the sin of the whole world. But God didn't only grieve over sin. He did something about it. Sin is the most expensive thing in the universe and God paid the price. He gave his own Son as a sacrifice to atone for the sins of the whole world. Man deserves to be punished for breaking God's laws, but God sent his Son to take the punishment we deserve.

If you are a person who suffers from a low self image, or if you are wounded emotionally, you face a great temptation to become self-centred. It is very easy to spend a lot of time feeling sorry for yourself, or thinking about your needs. Because of this, it is very important that you face the dangers of self-centredness honestly, and choose to put God at the centre of your life. You must aim to be more concerned about the pain God feels in his heart over man's selfishness, than the hurts you feel. By choosing to put God first in your life, you can break out of the patterns of manipulation, or self-pity, or fear that plague you. God longs for you to be healed of these hurts and the patterns they bring, but that cannot happen unless you replace yourself, as the centre of your life, with him as your Creator and heavenly Father.

God did not create us to live a selfish life, but to serve him and others. When we surrender to God we are set free to love others and ourselves, not in a selfish way, but with the same love that God has for us. He created us and cares for us—we are precious to him. As we know this kind of love, it frees us from being controlled by our own needs. Loving others, from a heart that is secure, keeps our love pure and untainted from manipulation and selfishness.

God's heart is broken by pride, hatred, bitterness, dishonesty, greed, and all other forms of selfishness. But in the same way *our* honesty, forgiveness, love, unselfishness and a desire to please him bring great joy to his heart—even more so because of all the selfishness in the world.

Have you ever experienced godly sorrow over sin? Let your anger turn to sorrow. Anger won't change you, but experiencing godly sorrow will. If you have never allowed your heart to be broken, then ask God to reveal to you your heart as he sees it. I am not talking about introspection, that is, looking into your past in a morbid way that produces condemnation, or a sense of failure. I am talking about hating sin the way God hates it, because you can see how destructive it is.

God's heart is broken over sin, and if you want to receive the Father's love, you must not presume on his kindness or breezily take him for granted. If my children want to experience my love when they have done something wrong, they don't do it by ignoring their wrong actions or taking my forgiveness for granted. Because I love them I want to make sure they are not being indifferent about what they have done. I long to put my arms around them and love them, but I love them enough to lead them to true repentance of things they do wrong. When they have been disobedient, or selfish, I take time to make sure they understand what they have done and why it is wrong, and then help them respond appropriately. When they acknowledge they are wrong and express genuine sorrow, then my love can be *received.* I give it regardless, but I have learned that when they are guilty for doing something they know is wrong, they are not really free to receive or enjoy my love and acceptance. I keep on giving it even though they are guilty, but because I love them I am not satisfied until they have received my love.

Many times we do things that are wrong because we are hurt, but that does not excuse us. Even if others have wronged us, we must deal with our attitudes and actions. Do we want to receive the Father's love? It will flood our minds and souls if we simply accept responsibility for what we have done or said or thought, and ask God for forgiveness. When we know we are wrong, we should take time to allow God to work in our hearts. We must not gloss over sin, no matter how small it seems. When we have done this *then* we can go on to receive his love.

Doing our part in this way makes it possible for us to receive the Father's love in full measure. I cannot heal myself, only God can do that. But I can acknowledge when I am wrong in a situation so that my focus is shifted away from blaming others, or justifying and pitying myself. When I do that, my focus naturally shifts to God. Then everything else can be right.

There was once a little boy who tore out a picture of the world from a Christian magazine, cut it into pieces and then tried to put it back together again. He eventually went in tears to his father because he couldn't put the world together! The father had watched his son and knew that on the other side of the picture of the world was a picture of Jesus. Then he helped his son turn over each piece of paper, keeping it in the same position, explaining to him that when Jesus is in the right place, then we can put the world together.

The Father's heart is broken over sin. If we allow our hearts to be broken with the things that break his heart, then he will be right at the centre of our lives. Then and only then can the world be put back together again.

5

GOD IS A LOVING FATHER

'What does God look like, Daddy?'

I can remember struggling one night several years ago with how to answer that question posed by my daughter, Misha, who was five years old at the time.

As I pondered over Misha's question, I realized that in her childlike simplicity she had asked a question that many people want answered. Perhaps adults state it differently, but the basic question is still the same. *If there is a God, what is he like?*

The Bible says that God is not a finite being like you and me, but he has made himself known to us in such a clear, understandable way that we can know what he is like: 'No one has ever seen God; the only Son ... he has made him known' (Jn 1:18).

I told my daughter what God looks like. I told her that he looks like Jesus. In fact, Jesus once said, 'He who has seen me has seen the Father' (Jn 14:9). Jesus is God in human form. We find many examples of how Jesus revealed the Father to us in the Bible. One example of this is found when some Jewish mothers wanted Jesus to bless their children, but his disciples thought he was too busy—too important to be bothered by these mothers. However, Jesus scolded his disciples and told them to bring the children to him. He took them in his arms and talked to them. He had time for them—to listen to their stories and hear about their games. He didn't mind getting dirty with little kids sitting on his lap—runny noses and all. Through seeing how Jesus had time for the little children, we learn that God has time for people. He cares, even about the little things in life. He is patient. *God the Father looks like his Son.*

God also looks like Jesus when he stopped to talk to the Samaritan woman by the well. 'What was so special about Jesus doing that?' you might ask. At the time of Christ, Samaritans were hated and despised by the Jewish people. They were looked down upon much like people in minority groups are in our society today. The woman he stopped to talk to was not only a Samaritan, she was a *woman*. In that culture and time, women were considered second-class citizens, and the Jewish faith did not respect women as equals or believe they could comprehend spiritual values.

Jesus elevated this woman to a place of equality and value, by the very fact that he broke social mores and was seen publicly talking with her. In doing so he showed us more of what God is like. God has created both men and women in his image. Both have equal value to him. And in discussing this woman's spiritual needs with her directly, he was not only demonstrating his concern for her person-ally, but he was also showing us by his actions that God the Father cares for men and women equally.

But not only was this lady a Samaritan woman, she was also a very loose, immoral woman, And Jesus knew that. Yet he was not ashamed to be seen with her. Just the opposite was true. He *wanted* to talk to her. That is why he went through Samaria: he wanted to take time to show *real love* to this woman who was known in the whole city of Samaria for her affairs with men. He saw beyond her hard exterior, the loud jokes, and the sarcasm about religion. He saw her heart. He saw her longing for something more, something that would fill the emptiness. He saw her need to be loved and cared for, to be someone special.

And she received his love. He helped her 'see' God in a way she had never seen him before. That is why Jesus came. He came to reveal *God* to us, and to bring *us* to God.

What does God look like? He looks like Jesus. I don't mean his physical features, for God is a Spirit, but through Jesus' love and concern for people we see what God is really like. As you read about the life of Jesus Christ in the Bible, it becomes clear that he was not just another religious guru. By his actions and words he demonstrated that he was a unique revelation of God. And not just God as the Jewish leaders of their day thought they knew God to be. Jesus spoke about God as his *Father*, a God who was *merciful* and *forgiving, kind* and *loving*. Yes, he is holy and righteous also, but many people have thought that if you believe God is holy, you cannot even so much as smile or act happy, and you can never wear brightly coloured clothes, or enjoy the arts, or love life! But the Bible reveals the true God, the God who created life, and has created it for us to enjoy! Jesus told his disciples: 'I came that they may have life, and have it abundantly' (Jn 10:10).

To call God 'Father' is difficult for some people. It seems they can call him anything but 'Papa' or 'Father'. They experience an emotional reaction that they themselves do not understand. There seems to be some kind of mental or emotional block to using the words 'Father' or 'Papa' in talking to or about God.

Why is this? I believe there could be several reasons. One is that some people have been taught all their lives that in order to respect God you must always address him as 'Thou'. They feel that to use informal terms in talking about God or to him is disrespectful. Such terminology may be good seventeenth-century English, but it is not biblical. The Bible teaches us to call God 'Father' when we pray (Mt 6:9), and that the Father wants to have a close, intimate relationship with us.

Other people cannot call God 'Father' in a spontaneous manner because they do not know him *personally*. The Bible teaches that there is a difference in knowing about God and *knowing* God in a personal way. In John 1:12, it says: 'To all who received him, who believed in his name, he gave power to become children of God.' This verse teaches that there are two things we must do to become children of God. Firstly, we must believe in his name. That means we believe that Jesus is the Son of God, that he died on the cross in order to take the punishment for our sins, and that he was raised from the dead as the Bible said he was. Secondly, we must receive him. That means we go beyond intellectual assent to actually praying and asking God to forgive us of our sins, and inviting Jesus Christ to be supreme in our lives. When we do these two things he becomes our Father in heaven.

Others still cannot freely call God 'Father' because of emotional wounds they carry with them from hurts in their relationships with their natural fathers. John Smith from

Melbourne, Australia tells about talking to a kid on the streets, a real street fighter, who gave John one chance to tell him about God. 'OK mate,' he said, 'what is God like?' Fresh from theological studies, John blurted out without much forethought, 'He is like a father.' The kid's eyes blazed with hatred and violence. 'If he is anything like my old man you can have him!' John found out later from a social worker that the kid's father had raped his sister repeatedly and beat his mother regularly.

Do you have those kinds of wounds in your relationship with your earthly father? Did he leave home for another woman? Did he totally abandon you as a child? Did he ignore you or compare you with others? Were you unwanted? Beaten or abused? Dominated or controlled? Perhaps you were pampered and spoiled to the point where you longed for discipline or guidelines for life?

Whatever the cause, if you cannot freely speak to God as your Father, I trust that as you read this book and as you study what the Bible says about God as a Father, you will grow closer to him and be able to call him your Father. If you are struggling to do that maybe you need healing from emotional wounds that make it difficult to trust God. God does heal wounded hearts.

Take François for example ....

6

WHY GOD HEALS
WOUNDED HEARTS

François took the French government to court to force
them to stop giving him money! Sounds incredible, doesn't
it? His story is one of the most unusual I have ever encoun-
tered, and illustrates the great love and power of God to
heal and transform a person's life.

He came to us several years ago when Sally and I lived
on the 'Ark' in Amsterdam. (The Ark is a Christian community, a kind of half-way house, that takes in people
suffering from life controlling problems. It was situated
at that time on two large houseboats that sat in the har-
bour behind the Central Train Station.) When I first saw
François, his eyes were unfocused and vacant, and his hair
was long, curly and unkempt. He spoke very little English.
After several hours, two of our French-speaking workers
were able to decipher his situation. He was using LSD and
morphine regularly, and he had been involved in a car accident which had rendered him permanently disabled due
to brain damage. He was also in a state of drug-induced
psychosis (which meant that he was totally out of touch
with reality due to his use of psychedelic drugs). We had
found him standing at the end of the pier next to our boats,

contemplating suicide. He had lost the desire to live and his ability to cope with reality as he knew it.

And no wonder: brain damage, family rejection, drugs, occult bondage, psychological problems—life offered no hope. The French government declared him incapacitated for life and gave him a monthly pension.

After ten months of prayer and fasting and many hundreds of hours of counselling and care, one of the young men who had committed himself to help François came to me and said, 'François wants to talk to you. He doesn't feel he should continue to receive the monthly pension the French government is giving him.'

'Why not?' I asked, a bit astounded at this latest turn of events.

'I think it is best if François explains it to you himself.'

The ensuing conversation has to be one of the most rewarding in the twenty or so years I have spent helping people out with their problems. In broken English, learned in the ten months he had lived with us on the Ark, François demonstrated to me just how deep the healing was that had taken place in his life.

He was thinking clearly, and not just about himself. He displayed Christian compassion and a desire to be a responsible person. How different this conversation was to the one I had had with him months earlier when he first came to the Ark! In those ten months, François had experienced freedom from occult bondage, and profound psychological and physical healing. This doesn't mean he was without problems or that he had worked through all the accumulated wounds of the past, but the healing he had experienced was real and, as the last eleven years have proved, it was permanent. During those ten months, François had come to the conclusion that life had meaning for him personally. He no longer wanted to die. In fact, he had developed a testy sort of stubbornness about life and what he wanted to do. He felt very definitely that he was to tell others about the forgiveness of sin, and wholeness of personality that he had found through putting his trust in Jesus Christ. He wanted to be an evangelist!

But first there was the little problem of the French government to deal with. François returned to France to tell the authorities he was not 'crazy', and that he could work as a responsible citizen to provide for himself. The authorities had never had anyone ask *not* to receive disability compensation. They felt sure he *must* be crazy!

So, they *refused* to stop sending François the monthly payments. But that did not deter him. After praying and seeking counsel from others, he decided to find a lawyer and take the French government to court, to force them to stop the disability compensation. Little did he imagine the surprises that were in store for him.

Some 'friends' of François contacted his lawyer and convinced him that it was in the 'best interest of all' that François should continue to receive his pension, and that he should testify against François in the trial. Much to François' surprise he did this. He was crestfallen. It was the last day of the hearing when things changed.

The judge called François to the bench to question him one more time.

'You say you are a Christian, young man?'

'Yes, sir.'

'And you believe that Jesus Christ has changed your life?' asked the judge.

'Yes, sir.'

'And you also believe he has healed you of your past problems, and you can work now?'

'Yes, sir.'

One more time the judge repeated the question, 'You believe in Jesus Christ as your personal Saviour, and that he has forgiven you of your sins?'

'Yes, sir.'

'Very good, young man. So do I! Case dismissed.'

The judge decided in favour of François. He too believed in Jesus Christ as his personal Saviour! Against unbelievable odds, particularly in France, God had seen to it that a Christian judge heard François' case. François was overjoyed. In spite of his past problems, and in spite of the efforts of disloyal friends and his own lawyer testifying against him, God had given him a victory. As a young Christian, François had seen God at work on his behalf as he did what was right.

This does not mean from that moment onwards François had no more problems. Although God does perform miracles of healing and restoration, he normally does this through a process, rather than instantaneously. God wants to involve us in the healing process. We must respond to God's love in obedience and humility for the healing to take place. This process is called 'sanctification'. (Sanctification means to make something clean that was dirty, in the sense of evil or selfishness; it also means to be set apart to be made pure or holy, to be made whole.)

It is very encouraging to see that the Bible speaks specifically about healing for damaged emotions. In the Old Testament book of Isaiah, the writer points to the future when God will send a Saviour to rescue people from their sin and selfishness. Isaiah 53:3 says that the Saviour will be 'a man of sorrows, and acquainted with grief'. It goes on to say that 'he has borne our griefs and carried our sorrows', and that 'with his stripes we are healed'. This healing is for both the guilt of our selfishness and the *consequences* of selfishness—the scars and wounds we bear in our personalities and emotions. In chapter 61 of the same book we are told that the Messiah, the Saviour, will 'bring good tidings to the afflicted ... bind up the brokenhearted ... proclaim liberty to the captives, and the opening of the prison to those who are bound'; and it says that those of us who mourn will be given the 'oil of gladness'. In Psalm 34:18 David says that 'The Lord is near to the brokenhearted, and saves the crushed in spirit'. The psalmist says in chapter 147:3 that the Lord 'heals the brokenhearted, and binds up their wounds'. *This is good news for a broken world.*

In spite of what Jesus has done for us, some people still wonder why God sits up in heaven, removed from the pain and harsh reality of this fallen world. They feel betrayed by God and they are bitter towards him because of that. 'Why has he created us and then abandoned us?' they question.

After being caught between two friends involved in a very hurtful disagreement, which brought to the surface some old wounds, one friend of mine found himself out in a field one night crying out to God, saying, 'I forgive you, I forgive you, I forgive you.' Until that point he had not realized that he had, quite mistakenly, been holding God responsible for what happened. In a way he was blaming God for the difficulties his friends were experiencing.

Don't many of us do the same thing? In our heart of hearts we often hold God responsible for the hurtful things people do to us, secretly nurturing the hidden feeling that, in the final analysis, he is to blame.

But God is not to blame. He is not the author of evil, nor does he tempt us with evil. He is just in all his ways, and kind in all he does. He is not the cause of our problems and he has not abandoned us in the midst of our problems. God came and lived among us. He became a man. He suffered all that we have gone through and much more.

God created man and man rejected him. God sent messengers and prophets to remind man that it was he who had created him but they stoned the prophets and killed the messengers. So finally God came himself. The Creator stepped into his creation, but the creatures refused to recognize their maker. In fact, the creatures crucified the Creator on a cross. What did the Creator do then? He turned this, the greatest of mankind's cruelties, around and made it the source of man's forgiveness! *We killed him and he used the act of our greatest selfishness to be the source of our forgiveness.*

Jesus Christ is the wounded healer. He has gone through all the pain and suffering that mankind has ever experienced. The Bible says that he was tempted in every way that we have been tempted. Speaking of Jesus, as a priest for us, the Bible says: 'We have not a high priest who is unable to sympathize with our weaknesses, but one who in every respect has been tempted as we are, yet without sinning. Let us then with confidence draw near to the throne of grace, that we may receive mercy and find grace to help in time of need' (Heb 4:15–16).

Do you hear what this is really saying? Do you see how different Jesus is from all those who have served in his name, but who have not cared for those they served? Jesus is in a class by himself. He is God, but a God we can come to freely, and a God who is not afraid to be involved with us. In fact, he has gone through what we have gone through so we would know for sure that he really loves us. He sat alone, abandoned by all his friends. He faced prejudice and deep rejection. He knew what it is to lose his father. He did not stay up in his holy heaven, far removed from the reality of this world. He came as one of us.

He was born into poverty. His race was ostracized and his home town ridiculed. He was not good-looking, and people questioned his friendships. His father died when he was young. In his latter years he travelled the streets and cities homeless. He was misunderstood in his ministry, and abandoned in death. He did all this for you and me. He did it to identify with us in weakness. But he also did it as a sacrificial act of suffering in our place, in order that we might be whole.

Jesus Christ, God's Son, came into the world to bring us healing and hope. We live in alienation because of our selfishness, and the selfishness of those who have sinned against us. We experience this alienation within ourselves, with God and with others. Jesus came to introduce reconciliation in place of alienation, healing in place of wounds, and wholeness in place of personality fragmentation.

The Bible also teaches that Jesus Christ is coming again. When he comes for the second time, he will culminate the healing and reconciliation process that he began for all mankind when he first came two thousand years ago. He will finish what he started. We can look forward to his second coming, because of the reality of his first coming. He will do away with suffering and sorrow, with sickness and disease, and with all selfishness. Then he will rule the earth with awesome power. But *now* he rules with patience and mercy. He has come to establish his rule, but he wishes to win men's hearts with love, not with force or might.

'His kingdom', that is, his rule in men's hearts, has come, but it is not fully here. The Bible promises that when he fully establishes his rule, all sickness, suffering and emotional pain will be done away with. We have begun to see those things now, but they will be fully realized when he returns again. They are substantial even now, but they will be complete then.

Why has he done it this way? Why hasn't he fully established his rule with all those promises fully realized *right now*? It is because he is seeking to establish his authority through our voluntary responses. He could use armies and absolute power to force men to serve him, but what good is it if we serve him out of fear, not love? That's not what he wants. He could use miracles and money to seduce us, but what good is it if we only serve him because of what we get from him, and not because we love him for who he is?

He is seeking to find the people that will fulfil his original intentions when he created mankind. *He wants friendship from us.* And he does not just want this with a collection of selfish individuals. His purpose is to unite all those who love him into a family. So whenever people love him he draws them together to enjoy deep friendship, mutual care and support, and celebration of the love, forgiveness and wholeness that he has given them. These family units are what the church is intended to be.

The 'Father's family' is also a channel of his love and healing to wounded people. As we love, accept and forgive one another, as God's children and as brothers and sisters, God's love flows through us to heal one another. Fellowship and friendship are one of the sacraments of the church. A sacrament has been traditionally defined as a means of grace. The sacraments include such things as baptism in water and the Lord's Supper. Through our brothers and sisters in God's family, God provides the kind of love and acceptance that frees us from our fears and allows us to grow into greater wholeness as people. We can be ourselves, and be committed to others without fear of rejection. We can accept others in spite of their weaknesses. We can forgive even when others hurt us. All of this is because of God's grace. It is his grace, that is his undeserved love, that does this for us. We don't have the ability within ourselves to be so loving. But God enables us to love that way. We don't have the ability within ourselves to heal one another, but through us God heals others. Every Christian has this ministry. We are 'grace givers'.

At this point it is important to bring a gentle warning. If we are wounded, we should be careful not to put our focus on people as the *source* of healing in our lives. People cannot give what only God can give. *If you want people to heal you, you will easily be disappointed.* Focus your attention on the heavenly Father, he is the only one capable of healing you totally. He will often do that *through* people, but remember that he is the source and people are the channel.

Emotional healing is almost always a process. It takes time. There is a very important reason for this. Our heavenly Father is not only wanting to free us from the pain of past wounds, he is also desirous of bringing us into maturity, both spiritually and emotionally. That takes time, because we need time to learn to make right choices. He loves us enough to take the months and years necessary to not only heal our wounds, but also build our character. Without growth of character we will get wounded again. We will do foolish, selfish things that will hurt us or provoke others to hurt us. Because he loves us he waits for us to want this kind of character growth. He waits for us to be ready to be healed. Often it is our right response to others that releases this healing into our lives.

How God heals wounded hearts

In the next chapter I have listed the steps involved in the healing of emotional and psychological wounds. I have not intended these steps to be treated as some sort of magic formula or talisman to wave in God's face. The truths that each one of these steps represent must be applied to our hearts as we are ready for them and with the guidance of God's Spirit. (If you don't know how to be guided by God's Spirit, ask him to help you. He has promised to help all those who ask him.) Take each step and apply it personally to your situation.

If your problems are complex you may need the help of a professional counsellor or psychiatrist. In the back of this book is an appendix with guidelines on how to choose a professional counsellor or psychiatrist. You have a right to ask them questions before you allow them to ask you questions. I think it is very important to stress that you should never submit yourself to being helped or counselled by someone, unless you feel very secure with them, and *very* confident that they are skilled and competent enough to help you. There is a world of difference between a Christian friend who tries to help you through encouragement and love, and someone who professes to be a 'counsellor', but is not qualified.

We don't have to live with pain. Because of God's love for us and because Jesus has suffered in our place, we don't have to carry our wounds with us all our lives. We can be healed and set free.

But there is a price to pay. I once met a man in India who wasn't willing to pay that price. In fact, he said something no other man has ever said to me. I met him one day in a market place in Southern India ....

7

HOW GOD HEALS WOUNDED HEARTS

I once met a man who said he had never sinned! It was in an open market-place in Madras, India. Because of our mutual interest in religion, our casual conversation quickly turned serious. When I shared that I believed God was basically forgiving to those who acknowledged their sinfulness, he asserted that he had never once done anything wrong in his entire life!

'You've never lied?' I asked him.

'No, never,' came the answer.

'You mean you've never stolen something or hated someone?'

'No, not ever once.'

'Have you committed adultery?'

'No.'

'Disobeyed your parents?'

'No.'

'Cheated in an exam at school?'

'No, not that either.'

I was baffled. Then I thought of another question. 'I bet you are proud of the fact that you have never sinned, aren't you?' I asked mischievously.

'Oh yes,' he replied, 'very proud, very proud!'

'There you are,' I said, 'you've just sinned for the first time! You are a proud man!' To which he laughed loudly and congratulated me that I had caught him in his only sin!

Though we are not all as proud as this man was, we have all ratified Adam's original sin. Adam denied God's right to rule over his life and chose to go his own way—and we have all done the same thing. It is hard for us to admit that we too have rebelled against God and denied his right to be God in our lives.

Without acknowledging this, the most basic of all mankind's problems (our selfishness), dealing with the wounds and unmet needs in our lives only postpones the inevitable. Pain-killers cannot keep a terminally ill cancer patient alive. They may take the pain away, and that is important when one is in pain, but why take the painkiller if there is a permanent cure for the cancer?

So it is with us, if we seek emotional pain-killers, but deny our most basic problem. Wonderfully, God longs to forgive us if we will only acknowledge our pride and selfishness and ask him to forgive us. Our deep, inner reactions to doing this should only confirm the truth of our need to do so.

By telling us that we have rebelled against him, God is not saying he condemns us or rejects us. Some people feel that God is rejecting them when they read in the Bible that they are sinners. That is not the case at all. God is simply helping us to understand the most basic problem we have and how to overcome it.

But we are not only sinners. We are also *sinned against*. There are things done to us, against us, by others, either intentionally through their selfishness or unintentionally simply because they are not perfect, that deeply affect us. Being sinned against, does not excuse wrong responses on our part, but it helps us to understand ourselves, and others, as we struggle to respond in the right way when we have been mistreated or hurt.

To gain the maximum healing and blessing, I suggest you go through the following steps slowly and prayerfully. Take time after reading each step to pray and apply it to your life. If it becomes painful ask a friend, or spiritual leader or someone he refers you to, to go through the steps with you. You need to be prepared for some pain if there are unhealed wounds. In order for them to heal properly, old wounds may need to be opened and cleansed of any 'infection', or bitterness that has set in. Even though it may be painful for a time, it will bring great joy and healing in the long run. Don't try to run away from facing your problems or you will only postpone the time when you need 'surgery'.

How God heals our wounds
Step 1: Acknowledge your need of healing

For most people this doesn't present a problem. But if we are wounded and do not acknowledge that we have a need, there is obviously no room for healing or help in our lives. To acknowledge our need is a sign of good mental health, as well as just being plain-old honest!

All of us need healing and growth in our emotions and personality. *Don't feel that you are an exception.* It is willingness to learn and humility that will allow God to work in your life. Some of us struggle with admitting our need, for fear of rejection. But the opposite is really true. When we admit our needs, others respect us more for our honesty. We can all recall a time when we made ourselves vulnerable and shared our needs, and then someone did not respond to us in love or wisdom. But don't let that experience keep you from the healing God wants to give you. Rise above the smallness of other people's actions. Don't let past rejection determine your actions or attitudes for the future.

Start by being honest with God. He knows everything anyway. He won't reject you. In fact, he is longing and waiting for you to be honest, so you can receive his love and help. Share everything with him. Tell him your hurts, fears, disappointments—*everything*. He loves honesty.

Then you need to open up to someone who can help you work through these steps of healing.

If you have wronged others you will need to go to them as well, and make it right. This is all part of acknowledging your needs. You do this not in order to be forgiven by God, but because you have been forgiven. The fruit of being in the right relationship with God is wanting to have broken relationships with others restored as well.

John Stott gives some very valuable cautions in this area in his book *Confess Your Sins*. He talks about the circle of confession: secret sins, private sins and public sins. We should only confess sins on the level they occurred. If it was a secret sin, that is, a sin of the heart or mind that was never acted or spoken out to others, then it only needs to be confessed to God. There is freedom of course to share these things with close friends or fellow Christians, out of a desire to be honest and to be accountable in areas of weakness in our lives, but we don't have to do that. That is our choice. In fact, we should only do it when we feel secure with others, and when we feel God is specifically leading us to do so, and never because we feel pressured to do so. Even then we must be wise and careful about how we share.

It could be very unwise to confess some sins of the heart to others. If it is our sin, and if the person we sinned against in our mind doesn't know it, we should not burden them with this sin, unless there is a clear reason why it will be helpful to them. If in doubt, mature counsel should be sought first.

There are some sins that are committed on the secret or private level of our lives that are shameful in nature. I believe we need to see a restoration of a sense of shame—particularly over sins of sexual impurity.

If you are in a meeting where *God* is leading people to confess their sins publicly, you should not feel pressure to confess publicly those things you have done in private. If you feel God wants you to say something, you can obey the Lord and at the same time be wise by simply saying, 'I have failed the Lord,' or, 'God has shown me how great his forgiveness is in spite of my past disobedience,' or, 'I have not lived up to the light I have had and God is showing me I have been a hypocrite. He wants me to confess that I have failed him, and I receive his forgiveness'.

Do not confess sexual sins in public under pressure from other people. If for no other reason it is unwise because you could present other people with temptations of unclean thoughts or burden them with impure pictures in their minds. People sitting in a group should not be burdened with confessions of someone's sexual sins without being asked if they want to hear such things. The very act of doing this can bring disgrace to the Lord, advertise sin, put pressure on others to feel that they too have to dig up their past sins and confess them. It may even lead people to confess things publicly that have not been put right with other individuals involved in the situation. At times it is helpful to share these things with a mature counsellor if we are struggling with condemnation and a feeling that God cannot forgive us, but we should not do that publicly.

If you must ask an individual to forgive you for sinning against them in this way, do not go into details or be unwise in your words. Say only what needs to be said. Confess that you have failed them or sinned against them and ask their forgiveness. That is enough.

A good rule of thumb to follow is if it is a secret sin, confess it to God; if it is a private sin, ask forgiveness of the one you have sinned against; and if it is a public sin, ask the group's forgiveness.

If you are weak in a particular area, it could be very helpful to share that with a few respected friends for the sake of accountability, but again, you should do it out of a sense of security and safety with these people and not because you feel pressured to do so.

To summarize, the steps to healing and wholeness, as related to honesty about our needs, go something like this:

(1) Be honest about needs and sins. Honesty about our needs or sins releases God's grace in our lives.

(2) Receive God's grace. Grace is God's gift of love, acceptance and forgiveness to us, and it makes us secure in him. That security releases faith in God in our hearts.

(3) Trust the Lord and others. Faith releases trust and makes it possible for us to have heart relationships with God and others.

(4) Build heart relationships with God and others. Relationships of love and trust with God and others are made possible because we have humbled ourselves. God can then release love and forgiveness both to us and in our hearts towards others.

The opposite of this process is also possible:

(1) Broken relationships. When relationships are broken we find it very difficult to trust others.

(2) Legalistic. When our relationship with others is wrong, we tend to become judgemental and critical. We live by 'law' not grace. This causes us to mistrust others.

(3) Mistrust. When we don't trust others we often project our mistrust which results in our feeling that others don't trust us. An atmosphere of rejection grows and walls come between us and others.

(4) Walls. Walls produce separation, the very opposite of heart relationships.

In looking at being honest about our needs, it is important to distinguish between a sin, a wound and a bondage. For sin there needs to be forgiveness, for a wound there needs to be healing, and for spiritual bondage we need to be set free. Sometimes we need help in all three areas. You cannot confess a wound as if it were a sin because a wound is not a sin. But if as a result of being hurt you have developed a sinful attitude or response, even if others are to blame, *God still holds you responsible for your response*. In fact, God does not see it as a matter of the other person being 80% to blame and you 20%, but both you and the other person are 100% responsible for your actions. Until you accept 100% responsibility for your actions, healing is blocked in your life. Why is that? If your attitude is one of resentment, bitterness, or an unforgiving attitude, God's healing and forgiveness are blocked. 'For if you forgive men their trespasses, your heavenly Father also will forgive you; but if you do not forgive men their trespasses, neither will your Father forgive your trespasses' (Mt 6:14–15).

To summarize this point, I cannot overstress the importance of acknowledging our need of healing if it is there in our lives. I have seen many people busy doing things for God, but their activity has been tainted by their need to prove themselves, or to gain acceptance, or by insecurity about what they were doing. Our service to God and to other people should flow out of our security and sense of well being, not out of a drive to prove ourselves or a need to 'be somebody'. In the long run we will please God, we will feel much better about ourselves, we will enjoy our work much more and we will be a greater blessing to others, if we take time to grow into wholeness and emotional healing.

Step 2: Confessing negative emotions

Some of us go through life collecting negative emotions. We were not taught by example how to identify or how to communicate our feelings, so we have stored negative feelings such as anger, disappointment, fear, bitterness and guilt since early childhood. Emotions that are not spoken out can be stored up inside us. Suppressing one emotion on top of another is like pushing one layer after another of rubbish into a plastic rubbish bag: something finally has to give. This process of building up unidentified and uncommunicated emotions produces terrible side effects. Everything from ulcers to suicide can result: we don't learn how to cope with difficulties, we grow up physically while our emotional development is retarded, and there is a great block to giving and receiving in our relationships with others and with God. Some of the major emotions that we often build up include rejection, anger, fear and guilt.

Dr Phil Blakely, a Christian psychologist, notes that to deal with this problem we need to 'decompact,' that is, to talk out the emotions built up inside us. To do this it is important to have someone to help us get our feelings out. For Christians, that should begin in prayer. If Jesus is not the one we turn to, before all others and above all others, we will never be healed. He is our Creator and our heavenly Father. He longs for us to share our feelings with him because he cares so deeply for us.

Of course, we need to talk to others as well. It is important to develop friendships with people who allow us to be ourselves, but who love us enough to challenge us when we are wrong.

Compacted emotions are not the root cause of our problems, but they can be a serious hindrance to recognizing and dealing with the root causes, and they can become a major problem in themselves if they are compacted internally over a long period of time. Of course communicating our emotions is not a panacea in itself. Communication of our feelings clears the channels so the root causes can be dealt with. If we communicate stored up feelings of guilt, that does not mean we have dealt with the causes of the guilt. This is where there is a major breakdown in relativistic psychology. To get people talking about their guilt feelings can make them feel better, but in the long run if one does not accept responsibility for violating God's moral laws, the feelings of guilt will return (unless of course a person completely sears his conscience and loses the ability to feel at all). Though emotions in themselves are not sinful, they can result in sinful attitudes if they are directed in a negative way towards God, ourselves, or others. That is where we need God's standards, as taught in the Bible, to be the measure for judging whether or not our emotions have become sinful. If they have become sinful we must treat them as both *unhealthy* and *wrong*.

God does not intend us to live by our feelings or for our feelings. Some people live by the axiom that if they feel good after something it is good, and if they feel bad, it is bad. That may be good existentialism, but it is not biblical Christianity. Truth as revealed to us in the Bible is to guide our lives, not feelings. God has given us the capacity for emotions and he intended them to be an encouragement for making right choices. If we do not live by God's laws, then we will twist his original intentions for emotions, and use them to reinforce a lifestyle of pleasure and selfishness. God did not give us the ability to experience emotions (feelings) so they would rule over us, but he gave them to us as servants for more godly living. Some people are totally ruled by their emotions, while others don't even know they have deeper feelings. They have suppressed their feelings to the point where they think it is very 'Christian' not to show any emotions at all. This is not being mature or 'spiritual'. God created us to live a balanced life where we express and enjoy our emotions, and where we are free to deal with them honestly and constructively, but he did not create us to be prisoners of our emotions.

Husbands, fathers, and spiritual leaders can be a great help to those they know, if they allow them the opportunity to share their feelings freely. Our desire to lead others can be ineffective or even harmful if those we lead are not given that opportunity. By creating room for those around us to be honest, we can lead them into a deeper relationship with God. Those we lead will trust us more and will sense our commitment to them, which in turn gives us the freedom to speak into their lives. Where there is no trust we have no authority. By giving people the opportunity to be honest we are 'giving grace', which in turn gives us the security to be honest about not only their emotions, but also the needs they have in their life.

If those we are leading have a serious mistrust of others, especially authority figures, it could be that they have never learned to express their feelings honestly in an atmosphere of love and acceptance.

My wife, Sally, once shared with me some personal problems she was experiencing. My response was to begin to give her advice on how to get out of the problem. I'll never forget her response to me. 'I didn't come to you so that you could exhort me or preach to me,' she said. 'I know what I need to do. When you exhort me it makes me feel as if you're not listening or caring. *I need someone to listen to me. If I can't talk to you, who can I go to?'*

I decided right then that I wanted to be the kind of husband who gave the freedom and security to my wife—and to others for that matter—to share their feelings with me without fear of judgement, sermonizing or reprisal. Of course I have also had to help others learn how to do that in such a way so that they are not negative or demanding.

To break this cycle of emotional suppression and mistrust, ask God to give you the opportunity to share with a figure of authority that gives you the freedom to be honest about your feelings. (And, of course, you must forgive those in the past who have not given you that freedom.) Your motive in sharing how you feel should not be to persuade others of your point of view, but to be honest.

However, honesty is not an end in itself. It is possible to be ruthlessly honest and at the same time be very cruel. If someone tells you all your faults in a cold, uncaring manner, totally unconcerned about the effect of their words on you, then their honesty is not virtuous but exactly the opposite: it is an expression of their great lack of love. And it is also possible for a sinner to be 'honest' about his sins but to show no remorse at all for his wrong-doing. The motive for being honest should be to become the person God wants you to be, not just the opportunity to vent your feelings or have a few nice relationships.

If we have been hurt by an authority figure or disagree with them, it is our responsibility to seek God first before we go to them. If we don't understand a decision they have made by praying about it, then we can ask them to clarify their point of view. We can feel free to disagree with a leader, but we shouldn't allow that to affect our attitude. We can disagree without becoming judgemental or breaking fellowship. Disunity never takes place because of disagreement. It is because we go beyond disagreeing to criticizing or judging someone. *There is no problem of unity that cannot be solved with greater humility or forgiveness.* God is concerned about our attitude of heart, as well as helping us grow by being open and honest about our feelings.

To summarize, it is important to communicate suppressed emotions. Keeping them inside can be very unhealthy, as well as leading to bad attitudes. But in getting them out, God wants us to accept responsibility for how we share our feelings and how we allow our feelings to affect our words, actions and attitudes. Honesty, together with responsibility for our actions, makes it possible to receive God's healing when we are suffering from emotional pain.

Step 3: Forgive those who have hurt you

Forgiveness is not forgetting a wrong that someone has committed against us, nor is it a mystical kind of spiritual feeling. It is simply pardoning the person for the wrong they have done. It is showing love and acceptance in spite of being hurt.

Forgiveness is often a process and not a once-only act. We keep on forgiving until the pain goes away. The deeper the wound the greater the forgiveness needed. Just as a doctor has to keep a physical wound in our bodies clean from infection so the wound can heal properly, so we must keep our emotional wounds clean of bitterness so they can heal. Forgiveness keeps the wounds clean. Whenever you think of a particular person and feel hurt, forgive them. It is not complicated. Just tell the Lord that you forgive that person, and that you choose to love them with God's love. Receive his love for them by faith. Keep doing that every time you think of the person, until you feel God's love released in your heart for them.

The motivation to exercise that forgiveness is God's forgiveness for us. If you find it difficult to forgive someone else, just think for a while about how much God has forgiven *you*. If it does not seem like a lot then you need to go further and ask God for a revelation of your heart as he sees it. Ask him to show the hardness of your heart. Ask God to do anything he needs, to break up the hard ground of your heart until it becomes soft with compassion. God will answer your prayer if you cry out to him sincerely and desperately.

Step 4: Receive forgiveness

If you have been hurt by others and have sinned in your reaction to them, it is important to not only forgive the ones who hurt you, but also to ask God for forgiveness for your wrong actions towards them. As you do this, you may discover a need to forgive yourself. At times our greatest enemy is our own sense of failure. We can often be much harder on ourselves than anyone else.

If you have failed, confess your sin to the Lord and then tell him that you receive his forgiveness and that you forgive yourself. Each time you feel that sense of failure returning, tell the Lord you do not receive it because he has forgiven you.

There is a difference between conviction of sin and condemnation. Condemnation is from a sense of failure. Conviction is because we have sinned. Conviction is specific and clear and from God; condemnation is vague and general and from ourselves or the enemy, Satan.

If you think you have sinned, but are not sure, ask God for conviction. If it does not come as you wait before him in prayer, thank him for his love and forgiveness and go on with your day. Remain open to him showing you any wrong attitude, but do not become paralysed by introspection. If God wants to show you any wrong attitudes, he is capable of doing so if you remain open to him. Do not wallow in the pigsty of self-pity. It is too destructive.

If you have wrong attitudes towards anyone who has hurt you, it is crucial that you confess this to God. But be careful: self-pity can be a counterfeit for real repentance. Dealing with our part in the matter often releases God's Spirit to work in the hearts of others. Even if this does not happen it is still our responsibility to keep our hearts right before God. If we become critical, hard-hearted, jealous, independent, proud, judgemental, unbroken in our heart attitude or bitter, *then we need to deal with our responses.* As we are broken before God then he will forgive us and heal our wounds.

There is healing through forgiveness!

Step 5: Receive the Father's love

There is a void in our lives that can only be filled by God himself. When you sin and ask for forgiveness, or you struggle with insecurity or inferiority, there is the possibility that that void is not full. Ask God at those times to fill you with his Spirit. Stand against self-consciousness with God-centredness. I cannot overstress the importance of this step in the healing process. *Self-pity and self-centredness grieve the Holy Spirit.* If you have grieved the Spirit of God, then you are not filled with his Spirit. Ask him to forgive you whenever you grieve him, and to fill you with his Holy Spirit. Receive the Spirit by faith (Eph 4:25–5:21).

As you do this, focus your thoughts and prayers on his character and on different aspects of his father heart. Worship him, that is, speak to him, sing to him, and think on him; concentrate on his faithfulness, his holiness, his purity, his compassion, his mercy, his forgiveness and his unchangeableness.

Developing an attitude of worship is one of the greatest keys I know to receiving the Father's love. Cultivate this trait above all others. Memorize scriptures or songs that you can use as weapons to combat loneliness or discouragement. Worship is the doorway that leads into the Father's presence. Worship is the pathway that leads you away from depression and self-pity. Some people say they cannot worship God when they don't feel like it because that would be hypocritical. My answer to that is that we don't worship God because of how we feel, but because of *who he is*. I often worship God *in spite of my feelings*. I don't want to be a prisoner of my feelings, so I praise God anyway. I try to be honest with God about how I'm feeling, but then I start to focus on who he is and not on how I feel.

Do you want to receive the Father's love? Then spend time in his presence. Receiving his love is not like receiving a piece of something; it is the result of being with God. We are bathed in his love as we spend time in his presence, giving to him. What do we give him? Through our words and thoughts we can give to him honour, adoration, attention, praise and worship.

If this is difficult for you I suggest you go through your Bible underlining the passages that specifically speak about the character of God. The Psalms are a good place to begin. Then pray and sing those passages to the Father in your times of prayer. As you do this daily you will find yourself growing in love with the Father. You will find him speaking intimately to you in response to your words of praise. Do not be surprised when he speaks words of appreciation, approval and love throughout the day. He loves to love his children!

Step 6: Think God's thoughts

In response to the hurtful things that are said and done to us, especially as children, we build destructive habits of thinking about ourselves. For example, if your parents were perfectionists and very demanding, you could have often failed to live up to their expectations. One way of responding to this could be to programme yourself for failure. If you 'know' you will fail, then you are in a way trying to protect yourself from disappointment. Unfortunately, if you think you will fail, you often will. Such negative thought patterns are often not accurate or kind. They are built on fear or are born out of rejection. If you think you are ugly, you will not only feel that way, you will also act that way.

The Bible says we should love God with all our heart, soul, mind and body, and that we should love our neighbour *as ourselves* (Lev 19:18, Mt 19:19). God wants us to love ourselves, not selfishly, but with his love. He wants us to think his thoughts about ourselves—thoughts of kindness, esteem, respect and trust.

If you have negative thought patterns about yourself, I would like you to stop now and write down the two or three negative ways of thinking that are most common. After you have done that, write down God's thoughts towards you that are the opposite of the negative thoughts, based on God's word or character. For example, if you wrote down that you think you will always fail, write opposite that 'I am good at ...' and name one thing you do well. Also write down what the Bible says about that area of your life. For example, 'I can do all things in him who strengthens me' (Phil 4:13). *Every time you start to think the negative thought, stop and say the positive thought along with the scripture.* It may take a long time to break a bad habit and replace it with a good one. Keep telling yourself the truth until you have broken the negative habit. Don't give in to lies and condemning thoughts. Persevere—with God's help you can do it. Cry out to him each time you fail, and start again. Have you ever noticed in the Bible how often God repeats something to somebody when he is trying to encourage them? In chapter 1 of the book of Joshua, the Lord tells Joshua *four* times not to be afraid. Why? Because Joshua needed to be encouraged to think God's thoughts about himself. He was getting ready to go into battle and he needed that encouragement. I am sure he must have repeated those words of the Lord to himself over and over again.

The most common cause of depression is thinking thoughts of depreciation and condemnation about ourselves. To break this cause of depression we need to follow the steps I have outlined above and then *get sick and tired of being tired and sick!* We need to break the habit of negative thinking by thinking God's thoughts.

This same principle also applies to reactions that go beyond our thoughts, to our actions. As you become aware of certain 'reaction patterns' in your life that are negative, defensive or selfish, write them down. Then beside them write down how God wants you to react in the situations that cause you to be threatened or defensive. When you find yourself acting in a negative or selfish way, stop and pray; then choose the way you know God wants you to respond.

In prayer, ask God to enable you to put these thoughts and choices into action. When you fail, ask for his forgiveness and keep going. If the devil tells you you have 'failed again' agree with him, but tell him you refuse to feel sorry for yourself! Accept responsibility for your failure, ask God's forgiveness or help, and continue doing this. Keep working away at it until you have established new habits of righteousness. It took you years to develop the negative habits, so don't give up because it takes a few weeks or months to replace them with God's habits. Start with one or two at a time, and then go on to others. As we do the possible, God will do the impossible.

Step 7: Endurance

Ninety per cent of success is finishing! The Bible says those 'who endure to the end will be saved' (Mt 10:22), and 'If we endure, we shall also reign with him' (2 Tim 2:12). Endurance has two aspects: on the one side it means the commitment on our part not to give up, a determination to go all the way through; on the other side it has to do with God's enablement. What God calls us to do, he gives us the grace to accomplish. His commands are at the same time his promise of victory. If he says, 'You shall be holy, for I am holy (1 Pet 1:16), that is not only a command, but also a promise—you *shall* be holy!

Sometimes you might feel it's impossible to go through to the end, to endure. And that may be right! But when we come to the end of what is possible for us, then we can see God do the impossible. Faith has not begun until we believe God for the impossible. We don't need faith to do what is possible. So if you are facing impossible situations in your life, praise God. Now you can begin to exercise your faith.

It is like climbing out on the limb of a tree for God, when you trust for something impossible. You are stepping out in a precarious situation where you know you need help. If you are overwhelmed with your needs or problems or the impossible situation you face, the devil loves to come along and tell you it won't work, that you cannot make it. 'The limb will break off,' he says repeatedly. So there you are out on that limb and what does the devil do? He starts cutting the limb off! He not only predicts it will break off, he tries to fulfil his own prediction! But stay right there and hang on to the Lord. When the devil cuts the limb off, the tree will fall on the devil and the limb will stay right up there in the air!

Why is endurance a step in God's healing process in our lives? It is giving up that allows us to give in to resentment, anger, hurt, rejection, lust, a critical nature, mistrust or whatever may be plaguing us. Sometimes we want God to perform a miracle and take away all our problems *right now*. But God is leading us in a process that is preparing us ultimately to reign with him in heaven. So we need to build character, and that comes through enduring difficulties or temptations and making the right choices.

Heaven is not just angels playing harps and living in big mansions. God wants us to rule with him. He has a part for each of us in ruling over his creation. But that begins in a relationship with him here on earth. The Father is preparing us as his children to share with him in ruling over all his creation. How will we do that? I don't know. But scriptures like the one in 2 Corinthians 4:16–18 confirm that God is preparing us for eternity: 'So we do not lose heart. Though our outer nature is wasting away, our inner nature is being renewed every day. For this slight momentary affliction is preparing for us an eternal weight of glory beyond all comparison.'

As a friend of mine says, 'It's how you finish that counts!' The apostle Paul says in his first letter to the Corinthian church, 'Do you not know that in a race all the runners compete, but only one receives the prize? So run that you may obtain it. Every athlete exercises self-control in all things. They do it to receive a perishable wreath, but we an imperishable. Well, I do not run aimlessly, I do not box as one beating the air; but I pommel my body and subdue it, lest after preaching to others I myself should be disqualified' (1 Cor 9:24–27).

There have been times when I have failed in an area of my life in which I am really struggling, and the devil comes along and says to me, 'You've failed again. You'll never make it. It's too difficult.' He tries to discourage me to the point of totally giving up.

Now if you stop to think about it, there is some truth in those thoughts. So I have learned to say to the enemy, 'That's right, I have failed again. But it is my responsibility. I accept my responsibility for what I have done. Thank you for reminding me of that. But I refuse to have self-pity over my failures. And you're right too, when you say I can't make it. By myself I cannot. But I can do all things through Christ who strengthens me. I am weak, but he is strong. Greater is he who is in me than you who are in the world.'

Then I rebuke him and his thoughts of defeat in the name of Jesus Christ and I begin to pray to the Lord. I confess my sin to the Lord and I refuse to feel sorry for myself. The cure for self-pity is confession of sin, turning away from the sin, and receiving the Lord's forgiveness.

As we confess our sins, turn away from them and choose to hate them as an act of faith, we receive God's forgiveness and God gives us a new beginning. *He is the God of new beginnings.* Our part is to humble ourselves and turn away from our sin or failure, his part is to forgive us and give us a new beginning. He loves to do that, because he is a God of love. It is pride not to receive his forgiveness if we have 'failed again'. If we've failed, we've failed; we must be honest and admit it, humble ourselves before God, and receive his forgiveness.

He is at work in you. *The struggle is part of the victory process.* You are learning lessons: you are learning to humble yourself; you are learning to receive forgiveness; you are learning endurance; you are learning from your mistakes and failures; you are learning how to help others and you are learning to fight the enemy.

We are at war! Don't give up! You are on the winning side!

And I am sure that he who began a good work in you will bring it to completion at the day of Jesus Christ .... Therefore, my beloved, as you have always obeyed, so now, not only as in my presence but much

more in my absence, work out your own salvation
with fear and trembling; for God is at work in you,
both to will and to work for his good pleasure I
can do all things in him who strengthens me ... and
my God will supply every need of yours according
to his riches in Christ Jesus .... Likewise the Spirit
helps us in our weakness; for we do not know how
to pray as we ought, but the Spirit himself inter-
cedes for us with sighs too deep for words .... What
then shall we say to this? If God is for us, who is
against us? He who did not spare his own Son but
gave him up for us all, will he not also give us all
things with him? .... Who shall separate us from
the love of Christ? Shall tribulation, or distress, or
persecution, or famine, or nakedness, or peril, or
sword? As it is written, 'For thy sake we are being
killed all the day long; we are regarded as sheep to
be slaughtered.' No, in all these things we are more
than conquerors through him who loved us. For
I am sure that neither death, nor life, nor angels,
nor principalities, nor things present, nor things to
come, nor powers, nor height, nor depth, nor anything else in all creation, will be able to separate us
from the love of God in Christ Jesus our Lord.

(Phil 1:6; 2:12–13; 4:13,19;
Rom 8:26, 31–32, 35–39)

8

THE SAUL SYNDROME

He was a tall, striking man. He carried himself with regal bearing and all eyes followed him when he passed through a crowd.

He had the ability to draw men to himself, to rally them to a cause and inspire them to greatness. Men had longed for a leader like this man. His very appearance convinced many that they could trust him. They had no fear of projecting on to this man their secret dreams and hopes. He was a leader's leader.

Or so they thought.

Underneath the broad shoulders of this tall, magnificent-looking leader, lay a heart that brooded with jealousy and fear. So deep were his insecurities, so uncertain the foundations of his personality, that any hint of greatness in others around him was perceived to be a serious threat to his position in the nation.

Unobserving men saw his natural charismatic ability to mobilize and communicate, but those who observed him more carefully noticed his total control of even the most insignificant tasks or persons. He trusted no one to do the job right, so his domination of those under him was almost unbearable.

His brilliance in battle strategy, his uncanny ability to do the right thing at the right time, convinced distant followers of his greatness, but only confused those close to him. 'He must be the Lord's anointed,' they thought. 'He always seems to be right.' They did not want to think the obvious: his violation of principle, his lack of servanthood, his unwillingness to promote others, his anger and impatience, all seemed to disqualify him from being King. In fact, they were deeply embarrassed and ashamed of his secret rages of anger and his fits of melancholy and depression. Was this behaviour fitting for a king?

But there was one man who was no longer confused about the character of this king. He was not impressed by his natural ability to lead. He looked for something more than just natural ability. He had watched to see if the King feared God and obeyed him in detail. He looked for humility and meekness, for righteousness, mercy and justice, but he didn't find these things.

And the irony of it all was that this man had put the King in office.

In a simple act of obedience, the prophet had poured oil on the King's head, prayed over him, and in so doing had installed this man to rule a nation. But the prophet, unlike many other men, was not impressed with man's 'power'. He had learned from early childhood that there was only one acceptable response to the voice of God: simple, child-like obedience.

And now his heart raged within him. Not in uncontrolled anger, but in righteous indignation. Enough was enough. He had waited patiently, watching the internal destruction of the kingdom due to the King's lack of integrity and obedience. He saw the deep insecurities of the King, the painful striving to find worth and security in the praise of his fellow men. He had agonized for countless nights over this man, in intercession and weeping. He had fasted many days, asking God to change the King's heart, and to help him find his security in the Lord's approval. But, alas, it was to no avail.

Now the word of the Lord had come to the prophet: 'I repent that I have made Saul king; for he has turned back from following me, and has not performed my commandments' (I Sam 15:10).

In a few moments of terrible confrontation it was done; the King's authority was taken from him. He remained in office, yes, but that was no guarantee of authority. Authority comes when God puts a man in office and places his anointing, his divine approval and enablement on that man. Power can come from a position, but authority comes from character, from obedience, and from God's anointing.

The prophet—whose name was Samuel—said to the King, 'Though you are little in your own eyes, are you not head of the tribes of Israel?' (I Sam 15:17).

What did these words mean, 'Though you are little in your own eyes ...'?

A closer study of the life of Saul reveals a pattern, a terrible, unmistakable pattern of inferiority and emotional hurt, independence, pride, and the fear of man. I call it the 'Saul Syndrome'.

He was 'little in his own eyes'. This is not to be mistaken as humility, for if that was the meaning of Samuel's words there would have been no need to remove Saul from

being King. Samuel was saying that even though Saul felt
inferior, that is, that he looked down on himself, he was
still responsible for all his actions before God. Inferiority is
never an excuse for disobedience.

In I Samuel 15, the characteristics of Saul's undealt
with inferiority complex are pointed out: *stubbornness and
independence*, ('rebellion is as the sin of divination, and
stubbornness is as iniquity and idolatry'—v 23), *pride*,
('Saul came to Carmel, and behold, he set up a monument
for himself'—v 12), the *fear of man*, ('I have sinned ...
because I feared the people and obeyed their voice'—v 24),
and *disobedience* ('Why then did you not obey the voice of
the Lord? To obey is better than sacrifice'—vv 19,22).
Simply illustrated, the Saul Syndrome looks like this:

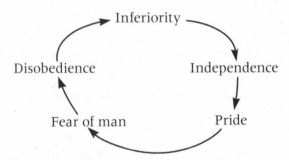

One problem leads to another. If we do not deal with
our emotional hurts in God's way it will lead us to independence, which in turn produces pride. Pride is much more
concerned about what people think of us, than what God
thinks of us, which results in the fear of man. The fear of
man inevitably leads to disobedience. We may still do a lot
for God, but it is a religion of dead works. Anything that is a
manifestation of insecurity, independence, fear of man and
disobedience, produces death in the long run.

Some of the most wounded people I know are also some of the most proud and independent. When we are wounded emotionally we are very susceptible to this vicious syndrome, that cripples even great men and women spiritually.

To help identify the Saul Syndrome, I have described some of the symptoms as they work themselves out in our daily lives.

1. Withdrawal or isolation. The Saul Syndrome leads us to cut ourselves off from others. Withdrawal can be a way of covering up or justifying our refusal to forgive those who have hurt us, or to co-operate with those with whom we disagree.

2. Divisiveness. It can cause us to be a source of division or disunity, particularly because we seek to get others to agree with us when there is disagreement or hurt. The Bible says that it is an abomination to God when we sow discord among brothers (Prov 6:19). Division is not caused by disagreement. There is no conflict between genuine Christians that cannot be solved by greater forgiveness or humility.

3. Possessiveness. The mentality of 'my ministry', 'my group', 'my opinion', 'my job', 'my place in the church' is selfish and comes from the sin of independence. The Bible teaches that rebellion is as the sin of divination—it comes from hell (I Sam 15). This is a 'me first' attitude and it is sin.

4. 'Us' and 'them' mentality. When we are caught up in the Saul Syndrome we start thinking in terms of 'us' and 'them'— those I agree with versus those I disagree with—instead of thinking in terms of all of us as one group or the whole body. It is a sign that we are not just disagreeing, but judging others, and that we are helping to create a faction in the church.

5. Manipulation. Proud and independent people can be manipulative by refusing to co-operate, demanding their own way, being critical, or constantly judging what others are doing. We spiritualize our reasons, of course, and that is why our manipulation can be all the more dangerous: we think it is being spiritual when it is really the very opposite. Some biblical scholars say that witchcraft boils down to using spiritual gifts to control others!

6. *Refusal to identify in spirit and attitude with the group or people we are a part of.* We justify our lack of identification because of disagreement, but real love and unity are not based on agreement anyway (unless it has to do with the doctrinal essentials of orthodox Christian faith). The real cause for our lack of identification and participation is pride and independence.

7. *Unteachableness.* The Saul Syndrome causes us to be closed to others. We refuse to receive correction and instruction. We become very hard.

8. *Being critical and judgemental.* When we stand off from the group we naturally tend to judge others and criticize them. We justify this in many ways, but it all boils down to slander and judging the motives of others.

9. *Impatience.* We think our way is better, and refuse to wait for others who don't agree or understand.

10. *Not passing on loyalty.* When we disagree with others in the body of Christ, or they hurt us, we withdraw from them, judge them in our hearts, and then tear down the respect of others for them as well. Or when someone else does this we all too easily receive criticism directed towards others without defending the ones being criticized or attacked. This is called taking up a reproach against our neighbour (Ps 15:3).

11. *Mistrust.* The Saul Syndrome results in mistrust. We accuse others of not trusting us, but that is often a projection of our own mistrust, and is a reflection of our reaction

to hurt or is a reflection of our independence. It has more to do with our needs than the needs of others.

12. Demanding attitude. We insist that others do it our way.

13. Disloyalty. Playing on the doubts, wounds or needs of others to win them to our point of view, rather than seeking to build unity, love, forgiveness and reconciliation, is another characteristic of the Saul Syndrome.

14. Ingratitude. We focus on what we think should be done for us instead of how much has already been done for us.

15. Idealism. We idolize a method, standard or programme and put them above people, particularly people we disagree with. Ideals become more important than unity or a right attitude of heart.

Even though the Saul Syndrome is often a symptom of hurt and unresolved feelings of rejection, it is still selfish and wrong and must be dealt with ruthlessly. *There is no problem of independence and inferiority that cannot be dealt with by greater humility and brokenness in our lives.* The Bible promises that as we humble ourselves, God will give us grace (Jas 4:6,7). We are afraid of humiliation, but that is not what the Bible means when it says to humble ourselves. Humility is the willingness to be known for who we really are and to take God's side against our own sin. Most people respect us *more*, not less, for humbling ourselves and confessing our needs. God *always* does.

If you are caught up in the Saul Syndrome, you will never be free until you accept your responsibility to repent of these wrong attitudes before God. It will do no good to blame others for your problems, or to make excuses for your sin. Humble yourself before God and others. Cry out to him in desperate prayer.

Many years ago I saw this pattern in my own life. I was hurting with deep insecurities, yet I was also very proud and independent. I longed for acceptance and affirmation, but was too proud to confess my desperate need for help. I was obsessed with what other people thought of me, particularly other leaders. It was only when I humbled myself before others and repented before God, that he delivered me from the Saul Syndrome. I covenanted with God that I wanted him to deal with these things in my life more than I wanted leadership, attention, or acceptance from others. I call it my 'Joseph-covenant'. I got alone with God one day in a forest in Holland and cried out to him. I told the Father that I wanted him *at any cost* to root out independence, pride and fear of man from my life. I told the Lord I could wait for as long as it took to happen, even twelve years like Joseph in Egypt, but I did not want to take any short cuts in getting my life right with him. That was a costly prayer, but I have never regretted it. God heard me that day and did a deep work in my life.

There is a difference between independence and being an individual. Each one of us is unique and in that sense we stand alone before God as an individual. There is a balance between the extremes of unhealthy emotional dependence on others and selfish independence. God's way is interdependence. That means that he wants us to grow into a *healthy* dependence on others. He created us to be social beings. He chose the family, a plurality of people, in which we are to grow and be nurtured into mature personhood, and he created the community of forgiven people, the church, in which we are to grow into spiritual maturity. He does not intend for us to be so emotionally dependent on others, either the family or the church, that we cannot function without being propped up by them, nor did he intend that we should live as emotional islands, cut off from others.

To meet this need of balanced emotional and social interaction, God has given us a family. In this family he is our Father and other forgiven people are our brothers and sisters. He delights in the coming together of his family for celebration of the love and forgiveness he has given us. This brings great joy to his heart. This family is the church. It is called by many names, and functions in many structures and cultures, but wherever his children come together in his name, he is with them; that is his promise.

Capitalism and communism are fallen man's efforts to emulate the 'Father's family' without moral content. Capitalism sacrifices the well-being of the group to the individual and makes the individual supreme. Communism does just the opposite: it sacrifices the individual for the good of the group, that is the state, and makes the state supreme. In God's family we are individually members of one another. As individuals we belong to each other. We are free to be unique individuals, not stamped in a mould to think, act or dress alike, but we also have the liberty to love and care for one another, to put each other first out of love. This balance of truth is found only in biblical Christianity—nowhere else. In this balance of truth there is great freedom. We are no longer slaves of our own insecurities or selfish desires. Christ sets us free, not to do what we want to do, but to do what we ought to do, to be what we were created to be. He sets us free to serve others and to receive their service to us.

However, we will never truly know this kind of freedom if we are dominated by the fear of man. The Bible says that the fear of man is a snare, a trap. How true! It imprisons us to the feelings and opinions of others. We are prisoners of fear, always worried about what others think, dominated by the actions of others instead of simply obeying God. Do you feel that you're always looking over your shoulder, trying to figure out why you are not included, or worrying when others get together, what they are saying about you? Are you determining your actions by how much approval it will bring from others rather than pleasing God? If so, you are bound by the fear of man.

The remedy for the fear of man is the fear of God! The fear of God is not an emotional fear, or fear of God's wrath or anything like that. The Bible defines the fear of God very specifically:

1. *The fear of God is hatred of sin.* Proverbs 8:13 says that 'the fear of the Lord is the hatred of evil'.

2. *Friendship and intimacy with the Lord are equated with the fear of the Lord.* Psalm 97:10 says, 'The Lord loves those who hate evil', and Psalm 25:14 says, 'The friendship of the Lord is for those who fear him'.

3. *The fear of the Lord is deep respect and awe of God.* 'Let all the earth fear the Lord, let all the inhabitants of the world stand in awe of him!' (Ps 33:8).

4. *The fear of the Lord is the beginning of wisdom and knowledge.* Proverbs 1:7 says, 'The fear of the Lord is the beginning of knowledge'.

The fear of the Lord is not some kind of holy look on your face, nor is it some sort of special tone in your voice when you pray, quivering like you have just come in out of the cold. The fear of the Lord is not a special feeling, a kind of 'liver-shiver', that comes over you. It is not your style of clothes, or the great number of rules you obey.

The fear of the Lord is to be impressed with God! It is more than simply respect. I respect the devil, but I am not impressed with him. The fear of the Lord is to love God so much that you hate all that he hates. This kind of hatred is not born out of religious neurosis, nor is it a reflection of our culture. It comes from being so close to God, so impressed with his character, that we love what he loves and hate what he hates. It is to allow our hearts to be broken like his is broken. The fear of the Lord is not a crusading anger, it is anger over the *destructiveness* of sin. It sees the cruel, deceptive, oppressive and destructive force of sin, and hates it for what it is.

The fear of the Lord does not happen by accident. It happens because we choose to fear him (Prov 1:28–29; 2:1–5), and give that top priority in our lives. It comes because we get sick and tired of being manipulated and controlled by the fear of man, and of being dominated by our fears and insecurities. It comes because we cry for it, we seek it, we search for it and we get desperate for it.

The Saul Syndrome can be broken, *you can be free*, but there is a price to pay. If you want inner healing and you want to know the Father's love, then you must choose the fear of the Lord. It says in Proverbs 14:26 that 'in the fear of the Lord one has strong confidence'. It is fear of the Lord and humility, that will bring us close to the father heart of God and release to us wholeness and self-worth.

9

FATHERS IN THE LORD

The world is filled with emotional and spiritual orphans.

Take Mehmet Ali Agca for example. Born in the remote mountain village of Yesiltepe in Turkey, Ali Agca was the eldest of three children. His father died when he was ten years old—and he smiled throughout the funeral. Ali hated his father passionately, and the violent scenes of his brutality were seared permanently in Ali's memory.

Shortly after his father's death he made a 'hate list' consisting of people and things that had become the focus of his hostility. Only out of consideration to his mother did Ali leave his father's name off the list.

Ali Agca grew up with fits of depression, accompanied by long periods of silence and withdrawal, and recurring anorexia nervosa. He suffered from guilt feelings because of the hostility he felt towards his father, and he ended up believing that hate was the only way to purge himself of these feelings. He was an orphan left without the knowledge of love.

As a teenager he followed a path of tragedy and crime: drug running, violence, and finally a school for terrorists in Lebanon for training people in the latest 'techniques of liberation'.

On May 13th, 1981 the trail of terror in Mehmet Ali Agca's life came to an abrupt end, but not before broadcasters throughout the world stumbled over the pronunciation of the unknown Turkish boy's difficult name. He became known as the man who had pointed his gun at Pope John Paul II and attempted to end his life.

Now Ali Agca sits in a bare, white-walled cell in Rome's Rebibbia prison. It was to this cell that John Paul made his dramatic pilgrimage of forgiveness in late December, 1983. Although on one level it was an intensely intimate transaction between two men, it was also an amazing example of Christian charity. John Paul sat for twenty-one minutes, holding the hand that had held the gun. Whether one is Protestant or Catholic, it is impossible to deny the significance of John Paul's actions. What he did was profoundly Christian. He sought out his enemy and forgave him.

In so doing, he gave Ali Agca a new understanding of God. In one simple act he offered him a way out of the darkness and bitterness of his soul; in those short twenty-one minutes John Paul, who said he spoke to Ali '... as a brother' opened up for him a way to the Father.

THE NEED FOR FATHERS AND MOTHERS IN THE LORD

There are so many people who are orphaned, not just from their physical parents, but who have been set adrift by a lack of spiritual and emotional roots. I have described earlier in this book the needs that many people have for healing. They have been pushed to the fringes of society by hurt and rejection and they are alone in the world.

It seems the church is also filled with many rootless, drifting spiritual orphans. Either they have been led to the Lord, but not cared for afterwards, or, because of some failure on their part or someone else's, they have not yet become part of a spiritual family. They need a church *home*, a place where they belong.

These people desperately need pastoral care. They need to be taught God's word, to be counselled with sound biblical principles, and to be encouraged and exhorted by someone mature in the Lord. They need a spiritual father or mother who can help them grow in the Lord.

Others need to be 'reparented', that is, given the kind of example that only a wise, stable mother or father figure can provide. When proper parenting is missing in a person's developing years, whether physically or spiritually, they still need someone to provide that example for them. It does not have to be an unhealthy kind of nagging, or 'hanging-on' to someone, but it is very important to have this basic need met.

BIBLICAL EXAMPLES

Peter exhorted the elders to 'tend the flock of God that is your charge' (I Pet 5:2), and Paul said to the Corinthian Christians: 'Though you have countless guides in Christ, you do not have many fathers ... Therefore I sent to you Timothy, my beloved and faithful child in the Lord, to remind you of my ways in Christ, as I teach them everywhere in every church' (I Cor 4:15, 17). Paul reminded the Thessalonians, 'We were gentle among you, like a nurse taking care of her children ... for you know how, like a father with his children, we exhorted each one of you and encouraged you and charged you to lead a life worthy of God' (I Thess 2:7, 11–12). Then there is the warning God gave the 'shepherds of Israel' in Ezekiel 34. It leaves no doubt as to what God thinks when there is no one among his people to feed the sheep, strengthen the weak, heal the sick, bring back the lost and gather those who have scattered and gone astray.

Being a father or mother in the Lord is not limited to those who are pastors or spiritual leaders. There is also a very crucial role for those who have come into the maturity of 'fathers' or 'mothers', who do not necessarily have a public leadership role in the church, but who have a heart to care for others. Speaking of those who are fathers in the Lord, John says, 'You know him who is from the beginning' (I Jn 2:14). Young men like to fight the devil, but fathers know the Father. By their very presence, they minister to those around them because of their maturity and depth in God. We need to turn these mums and dads loose in the church to be who they are. By being available, having time for people and having an open home, their lives minister healing and love.

THE NEED FOR BALANCE

As in everything, the emphasis on fathers can be carried to an extreme. The last thing people need today is abusive authority. The Bible speaks of equality, authority and ministry. It is very important to distinguish the difference between these three concepts. Much confusion has resulted in the body of Christ because the proper distinctions have not been made.

Godly fathers want to serve others, and treat all men and women as their equals. They start with an attitude of equality, not of authority, because they are more concerned with serving than authority. When you begin with an attitude of authority, it is bound to result in a feeling of superiority, or a kind of paternalism that can become dominating and suffocating for others.

I think it was that kind of domineering authority that Jesus had in mind when he said in Matthew 23:9, 'Call no man your father ....' In fact, the context of Jesus' statement is a warning about pharisaism. He was condemning those who lead out of pride, who 'do all their deeds to be seen by men'. He was not saying we do not need fathers in the Lord. Just the opposite is true. He was saying a true leader leads as a loving father and not a master or someone we put on a pedestal. So it is not the title we give a spiritual leader that is important—Jesus used three different titles in Matthew 23:1–12 to illustrate his point—but it is the attitude of those behind the title. You can call a leader 'servant', but if he is a dictator then the word will soon lose its true meaning. Perhaps the whole point of what Jesus was saying is that godly authority is not dependent on the title we have or the position we hold, but whether or not we have a servant attitude and we are truly humble in the way we relate to others.

Perhaps the following chart will help point out the differences between the two approaches. (See also Appendix B.)

Dominating Fathers

1. Function as if *they* are the source of guidance for people's lives.

2. Emphasize the *rights* of leaders.

3. Set leaders apart from the people with special privileges.

4. Seek to control people's actions.

5. Emphasize the importance of leaders ministering to others.

6. Use rules and laws to control people and force them to conform to a 'mould'.

7. Confront sin on the level of outward actions and group conformity.

8. Stress the uniqueness of their group, and the special revelation God has given to their group and not others.

9. Judge people's responses to God on how consistently they see things from the leaders' point of view. Discourage diversity of thought and action.

Fathers in the Lord

1. Believe God is the source of guidance and other Christians should learn to hear his voice for themselves.

2. Emphasize the *responsibilities* of leaders.

3. Emphasize the body of Christ serving one another, with the Lord the centre of attention.

4. Encourage people to be dependent on God.

5. Emphasize the importance of equipping the saints for the work of the ministry.

6. Provide an atmosphere of trust and grace to encourage spiritual growth.

7. Confront sin on the level of heart attitude and brokenness before God.

8. Stress the importance of unity within the whole body of Christ and the importance of keeping a humble attitude towards others.

9. Stress the importance of heart attitude to God and not just doctrinal conformity as a basis of unity.

Biblical authority is never taken, it is offered. Authority is not a position or a right. It is the outworking of who we are, not an office we hold or a title on our door. It comes from the anointing of God's Spirit and is the sum total of a person's character, wisdom, spiritual gifts and servant attitude. In order for authority to work in a biblical manner it must be accepted, that is, if a person does not receive what a leader says, the leader has no authority in that person's life, whether the leader is right or wrong in what he is saying. To try and force it to be otherwise leads to manipulation and coercion.

Fathers in the Lord understand these principles about authority. They know the character of the Father so they are relaxed in their ministry to others. This doesn't mean they are not firm or they cannot confront people when necessary, it is just that they have learned to do that because it is what the Father would have them do, and not because they are 'the leader'.

RECEIVING FROM FATHERS IN THE LORD

It takes humility to receive from someone. When God brings a person into our lives that he wants to use as an example and to give counsel, we must be in the right attitude in order to receive all that God has for us through that person.

God longs to comfort us and encourage us through others, but he cannot do that if we don't have a teachable attitude—a heart that is open to receive what he wants to give us. It is not a sign of humility or maturity if we think we do not need to receive from others—it is *pride*. Of course, we have the final responsibility before God to discern if what others say to us is right for us. We cannot agree with people if we do not have the conviction they are right.

There is a difference between having a submissive spirit, and absolute obedience. Absolute obedience is only given to God, submission is given to man. Submission is an attitude of openness to receive from someone else. God is the only one worthy of total allegiance.

When several of David's 'mighty men' (brave men in his army), overheard him say that he longed for a drink of water from the wells of Bethlehem, they decided to get it for him. There was only one problem—the wells were within the Philistines' camp—David's enemies. So they fought their way into the camp on a daring raid, risking their lives to get David some of that precious, cold well water.

Can you imagine the looks on their faces when they staggered back into the camp, wounded and bleeding, but ever so proud of themselves for their accomplishment? Then to their great amazement, David took the water they offered to him and poured it on the ground! 'Devotion such as this,' said David, 'belongs only to the Lord.'

David refused to receive this kind of loyalty and commitment. It belonged only to God, not man! Yes, his men were deeply loyal to him, but David knew that there was the capacity in men's hearts for a kind of devotion that was only to be given to God, so he rightly redirected this sense of devotion in his men to God. Hurt as they must have been, years later those same mighty men told others the lesson David had taught them, how he had made it so clear to them that God must always be first in their lives. In the long run they respected David more for what he did.

To be 'fathered' or 'mothered' in the Lord, does not mean we have to have a formal, defined relationship with a mature Christian. Sometimes it just means watching their lives. Other times it means asking questions or seeking counsel.

Jesus fathered his disciples in four stages:

1. He did it and they watched.
2. He did it and they helped.
3. They did it and he helped.
4. They did it and he left!

FATHERING OTHERS

Being a good father, whether in the church or the home, has more to do with the atmosphere we create than the words we speak. People will remember our attitudes and actions, *how* we say things, far longer than the actual words we speak. Those attitudes, and our underlying philosophy of life and ministry, create an atmosphere everywhere we go. We bring it with us.

For example, when you are with some people, it is not long before you know they care about you. They convey it in many little but obvious ways. It isn't long before you feel free to be really open and honest with such people. Whereas with others, you wouldn't tell them something personal, even if they swore on a thousand Bibles that they would not tell anyone else.

I believe being a father or mother in the Lord to others has more to do with who we are than what we do. It is the kind of atmosphere we create. Obviously, it is important to be more specific than to just say we should create a nice atmosphere, or all we would need to do is burn some nice candles, play the right music, and then we'll have a 'spiritual atmosphere'. By spiritual atmosphere I mean the life principles we convey by our words and actions. That does not happen by accident. It is the result of our whole lives.

Some enemies of Charles Finney, the great nineteenth-century evangelist, tried to embarrass him on one occasion by asking him to speak at a large pastor's conference without prior warning. Finney graciously accepted their last minute invitation and gave a powerful message for one and a half hours! Afterwards a young student asked him how long it had taken him to prepare his sermon. 'Young man,' Finney replied, 'I have been preparing that sermon for the last twenty years!'

Listed below are some of the ingredients that contribute to an atmosphere of love and trust.

> We create an atmosphere for spiritual growth by our love and trust towards others.
>
> We create an atmosphere of friendship by our availability to others.
>
> We create an atmosphere of belonging by including others in important decisions.
>
> We create an atmosphere of responsibility by trusting others.
>
> We create an atmosphere of compassion by our courtesy and kindness to others.
>
> We create an atmosphere of godliness and spiritual reality by meditating regularly on God's word, and by being a personal worshipper of God.

We create an atmosphere of faith and vision by seeing needs and discerning God's response to the need.

We create an atmosphere of generosity by constantly giving to others.

We create an atmosphere of righteousness by acknowledging God's enablement in every situation.

We create an atmosphere of human value and worth by having time to listen to others.

We create an atmosphere of self-esteem by constantly affirming and encouraging others.

We create an atmosphere of God's nearness by total openness to the person of the Holy Spirit.

We create an atmosphere of comfort by caring when others are hurt.

We create an atmosphere of team unity by sincerely desiring to release others into their ministry in God's timing; we sincerely pray that their works will be greater than ours.

We create an atmosphere of joy and peace by constantly expressing our thankfulness and gratefulness to God in every situation.

We create an atmosphere of security by seeing the good and the potential in others.

We create an atmosphere of obedience to God by fearing him and not fearing man.

We create an atmosphere of loyalty by never being critical of others.

We create an atmosphere of faith by being impressed with the greatness of God.

We create an atmosphere of honesty by being transparent, and admitting our own faults and weakness and asking for forgiveness when we have wronged those around us.

If we, as parents or spiritual leaders, have hurt our children or those we lead, we should pray seriously about making restitution. They need to hear us say we are sorry and we need to hear them say we are forgiven. It is not enough to 'let bygones be bygones'. If we do humble ourselves in this manner, it often opens the door to healing and reconciliation and makes the deepening of our relationships possible.

What greater inheritance can a father and mother give to their children? Our greatest gift is our love and humility. If we do this, we are teaching by our lives the truth of God's word. We are creating an atmosphere of grace and we are building a highway of love between our hearts and the hearts of others. Not only does this make heart relationships possible between ourselves and others, but it also makes the father heart of God a reality.

10
DEALING WITH DISAPPOINTMENT

It was a great moment in the nation's history. After many long years of national strife and civil war, the nation was once again united, its enemies to the south were finally defeated, and now, most important of all, after twenty long years of spiritual barrenness, worship was being restored in the new capital of that united kingdom. Saul's rule was over (having ended in his death on the battlefield). Young David was now the leader, and there was an air of expectancy throughout the land. It had been a long night and the dawn was now breaking.

David had declared to the nation that he was bringing the ark of the Lord back to Jerusalem. Tens of thousands of people gathered in the city of the kings to celebrate this momentous occasion. Every family and tribe was represented, and the throngs of people were alive with excitement and expectation.

Young David the King was overwhelmed with joy. He thought God must have been pleased now that his people were united, and he felt that they could worship the Lord once again.

'And David and all the house of Israel were making merry before the Lord with all their might, with songs and lyres and harps and tambourines and castanets and cymbals' (2 Sam 6:5).

Then, suddenly, without warning, tragedy struck. The oxen stumbled, and when young Uzzah put out his hand to steady the ark—he fell to the ground dead. David saw it happen and was stunned. What did this mean? The whole multitude of people grew silent as word of what had happened spread through the crowd.

David was angry, embarrassed and afraid all at the same time. He wondered why this had happened, when he was doing as the Lord commanded. Uzzah had only touched the ark ....

Though David was confused, he knew one thing for sure: he could not proceed with the ark until he knew why God had judged his actions. But he was *deeply disappointed*. If only he knew why—what had he done to displease the Lord?

Can you imagine the disappointment David experienced as he walked home all alone? It had started off as such a beautiful day, and now, in the midst of it all, such disappointment. No doubt he wrestled with feelings of personal failure and condemnation, and at the same time struggled with the anger he felt towards God.

'And David was angry because the Lord had broken forth upon Uzzah; and that place is called Perez-Uzzah, to this day. And David was afraid of the Lord that day; and he said, "How can the ark of the Lord come to me?"' (2 Sam 6:8–9).

Most of us can identify with David. At one time or another in our lives, we have felt God telling us to do something so we have stepped out in faith and obedience, only to find it going wrong. 'Why?' we ask ourselves. We are trying to obey God; why is it going wrong? Have you ever found yourself in such a situation? Hurt and confused because of disappointment?

Perhaps it was not so much that you were stepping out in an act of obedience to God, but just disappointed because of the circumstances in which you found yourself. Did others let you down? Were you hurt by someone close to you and disappointed in their actions? Maybe you had expectations that were not fulfilled, or you do not understand why a promise of the Lord to you did not come to pass?

Disappointment brings the potential for hurt, discouragement, bitterness, anger, doubt and fear. If the disappointment is great, its effects can linger with us for months or years. That is why it is so important to learn to deal with disappointment.

THE ETERNAL NATURE OF DISAPPOINTMENT

Paul Billheimer points out in his book *Don't Waste Your Sorrows* (Kingsway Publications 1983), that our disappointments can be a source of great blessing if we respond to them in the right way. Nothing can injure us emotionally, unless it causes us to respond with the wrong attitude. It is our response to disappointment that either hurts us or helps us. The eternal nature of a thing is not in the thing itself, but in our reaction to it. The disappointing circumstances will pass, but one's reaction to them will release a moral and spiritual deposit that will last for ever.

As long as there are people, there will be disappointments in life. A friend of mine once said, 'We're going to have unity around here even if I'm the only one left!' Dealing with disappointment is learning to deal with people's weaknesses. It is developing patience and flexibility, and understanding of God's ways. It is learning to respond as God would have us to, in every circumstance. That does not mean becoming a doormat in life, but it does mean learning to respond with a Christlike attitude to those who want to treat you like one!

LEARNING TO EAT IN PEACE

Christians learning to love and accept one another is rather like brothers and sisters learning to eat their dinner together without arguing. I can remember getting really angry with my sister Judy and my brother Alan at the family dinner-time. I also learned that arguing at mealtimes was something my father would not tolerate! He insisted we learn to eat together in peace.

I can also remember times when my younger brother, Alan, and I argued together, but when we went to school I would defend him with my life if any of the other children gave him any trouble! Don't we, in God's family, tend to be that way as well?

Some of our disappointments come because our expectations for each other are too high. Becoming a Christian does not mean you and everyone else are suddenly going to be perfect. We need to *learn* to love our brothers and sisters, just as we have to learn to eat in peace.

When we are disappointed in the actions of a brother or sister, we mustn't turn them away, or cut them off from further fellowship. Perhaps God has brought them into our lives to teach us something. The psalmist David said, '… in faithfulness thou hast afflicted me' (Ps 119:75).

Perhaps the very people we thought were an attack from the devil, are a loving 'affliction' from the Lord—to teach us to be more loving and patient! Besides, if you and I were as loving as we thought we were, there would be no problem in responding to difficult people. If our hearts were filled with nothing but love, we would always respond lovingly! I am sure God allows, even arranges sometimes, the difficult experiences we go through, so that our character weaknesses and wrong attitudes are brought out in the open for him to deal with.

Cultivating humility

King David learned to deal with his disappointing experience when Uzzah lost his life, but it required a great act of humility on his part. He could have hardened his heart in pride, and blamed God for what happened. Instead, he sought God to find out what he had done wrong, and what God was teaching him in the situation. David learned above all things to humble himself, in order to find out what God was wanting to teach him.

Humility is not only being honest, but it is agreeing with God in how he sees a situation. Many people are ruthlessly honest, but they don't go on to take God's side against sin, and to have God's attitude towards the sinner. Both are necessary if we are to learn from the disappointments of life.

Obviously there is a need for comfort and understanding during times of disappointment, especially if it involves tragedy or loss of life, but for those circumstances where there is relationship conflict, or we feel God has let us down, then we must humble ourselves before God so that we can receive grace *to go through the difficulty* and grace to learn what God wants to teach from the difficulty.

For the person who learns to go to God and ask him
why he allowed a situation to take place, or what he wants
to teach them through it, disappointments bring tremendous growth and spiritual understanding. On the other
hand, pride is the greatest hindrance to learning through
difficulty and disappointment. Pride is our greatest barrier
to spiritual growth. Overcoming pride is the key to gain-
ing victory and understanding, when we are disappointed.
Consider these symptoms of pride and how they can hinder
us in responding in the right way:

... Pride sees the wrongs of others, but never identifies
with others in weakness. It never says, 'Yes, I've done that
too,' or 'I understand. If it were not for God's grace I would
have done that also'.

... Pride does not admit wrong or personal responsibility, or if it does, it excuses it and explains it away to the
point where there is no sorrow for the wrong done.

... Pride is occupied with blaming others, with criticizing and pointing out why others are wrong.

... Pride produces hardness, arrogance, self-sufficiency
and independence.

... Pride is more interested in being right in the eyes of
others, than being good in the eyes of the Lord.

... Pride is more concerned with winning arguments
than with keeping friends.

... Pride never says the words, 'I am wrong. It is my
fault. Will you forgive me?'

... Pride makes us feel that we are more spiritual or
closer to God than others. It results in our feeling justified
in thinking that we are too good to be identified publicly
with certain groups or individuals.

... Pride produces a demanding spirit. It focuses on what has not been done for us rather than what has been done for us. It covets the past or the future, but is never satisfied with the present.

... Pride results in ungratefulness. Pride says, 'I deserve more, or better'. Pride does not believe it deserves hell.

... Pride justifies avoiding or ignoring others.

... Pride is divisive. Pride causes us to compare ourselves with others and results in our looking down on others. Pride says 'my' group (or church or denomination) has more truth than others.

... Pride lends itself to an unteachable and uncorrectable attitude.

... Pride causes us to judge situations by what they mean to us and not to God. Pride cannot see God's perspective in a person's life or a group.

... Pride results in a negative, judgemental and critical attitude, slander and back-biting. Pride gossips, tears down, ruins reputations and delights in spreading news of failure and sin.

... Pride blames God and others when things go wrong.

... Pride excuses bitterness and resentment.

... Pride leads to pity, pity and more pity.

... Pride says we can reach a level or depth of spirituality where we are finally free of pride, and results in us putting our security in a most grotesque form of self-righteousness, and not in the cross of Jesus Christ.

It was in the most painful, disappointing experience of my life that I learned about pride: my own pride, and the pride of others.

I never imagined it would happen to me. I had heard of divisions and church splits and deep, tearing conflicts between people, but it never entered my mind to think that it would happen to me.

In fact, we had put such an emphasis on relationships and unity, on being a 'family' and loving one another, that I was proud of the fact that we were on the 'cutting edge' of the church. I saw other groups and despised them (I didn't see it as that then) for their superficiality and lack of personal warmth. I couldn't imagine being publicly identified with some parts of the body of Christ because of their crassness in evangelism or their lack of radical discipleship.

I taught on priorities in the body of Christ, on vulnerability and loyalty. I felt strongly about the church being a *community* of believers, of the importance of availability and quality of relationships. I stressed life-style and the kingdom of God and justice. In fact, I still teach on these things, but ten years ago I taught them to such an extreme that Jesus was no longer the centre of my life: other believers were.

That was the big problem of course. We were a community of people that had become infatuated with ourselves: we saw ourselves as unique, and when that happens you are in for big problems.

We had set such high standards for ourselves, not only was it impossible for other believers to live up to them—we couldn't either.

So we turned on each other. Christmas Day 1975 was the saddest day of my life. I found myself sitting on my bed that morning contemplating my shattered dreams: I had dreamt of a loving community of people living the gospel so radically that we would shake the world. But it seems that I had not calculated the fallenness of man into my equation for success. So dreadful was our failure, so hurt was I by my own sin and the sin of others, that I despaired of life itself.

That shook me. I had never seen myself as weak. But here I was thinking of suicide as a way to escape pain and disappointment.

I was disappointed in myself, in others—even in God. Why had he let this happen? Why hadn't he warned me? Why had friends let me down? Why had people accused me behind my back?

I cannot describe the pain. I felt crushed, rejected, betrayed, and at times angry, hostile to the very people I loved so much. Our little paradise of love and healing relationships had turned for a brief moment into a hell of broken relationships, the brutal reality of being left without God's grace to restrain us from being who we really were without him.

The leadership was divided. Our fellowship was split. People took sides. And there were meetings. So many of them I was sick of them. We met all together to talk about our problems, and we met in homes to talk about each other. Then we had meetings to discuss the meetings. So many unnecessary, hurtful words. So much mistrust and accusation.

I now look back on those terrible dark months with great thankfulness to God. It was the most painful period of my life—and the best. God did more in those days of division and shattered dreams to show me myself, my deep insecurities and my pride and independence than I had seen in the rest of my life put together. And correspondingly, he showed me more of his mercy and love and faithfulness than I ever dreamed possible.

Because of the pain that I experienced in those days, and the healing and redemption that came as I humbled myself before God and others, I learned many lessons. I learned so much about God. When the breakthrough finally came in my own life personally, it came as God revealed to me the root of my own wrong attitudes towards others; then for two hours wave after wave of God's mercy flooded over me. I wept with deep sobs as I heard him gently whisper into my mind, 'I forgive you, and I restore to you all that has been lost'.

Because of that experience I have a greater awareness of the danger of pride, and a deep tenderness for those who have experienced hurt and disappointment, especially through relationship conflicts.

I recognize that we don't have to experience each person's problems personally to be able to identify with them. True identification with others comes from the Holy Spirit, not an emotional sympathy. Jesus never sinned, but he understands sinners better than anyone else. But going through hurts and disappointments can make us much softer and more tender to the needs of others, if we respond rightly to what we have experienced.

David humbled himself. In fact, he did it again and again. That is why the Bible says he was a 'man after God's own heart'. It was David who wrote in Psalm 51:17, 'The sacrifice acceptable to God is a broken spirit; a broken and contrite heart, O God, thou wilt not despise'.

Brokenness to David was not despair, or hopelessness, or being hurt. It was humility—the opposite of pride.

Because of that, David learned from every disappointment in life. His beautiful psalms of praise were learned in the crucible of life's disappointments.

Do we want to learn to trust God as David did?

To do that we will need to learn to humble ourselves as David did. When things go wrong we can either humble ourselves, or become hard and proud. There is no middle ground. A mixture of humility and hardness will not bring the results God desires. Even if we have done nothing wrong in a situation, we still need to learn to forgive and to bless our enemies, and that can only happen if we have humble hearts.

Below are some simple principles I have learned that have been helpful in dealing with disappointment. I have put them in the form of questions to ask myself.

1. Lord, what do you want to teach me in this situation? What attitude should I have? What should my response be? What biblical principles, if any, have I violated in this situation?

2. Has there been any disobedience in doing the right thing? Has the timing been right, the correct method used, and the right people involved?

3. Do I need to forgive anyone in this disappointment?

4. Do I need to seek the counsel of any godly person for help in this situation?

5. Am I overspiritualizing this situation and missing some practical lessons?

6. What are the adjustments and changes I need to make?

7. Who should I now be serving, instead of being worried about myself?

It is difficult for some people to internalize the lessons of life. If we were brought up without the example of godly parents or without wise, loving discipline, applying lessons from disappointments or difficulties can be very difficult and threatening. If that is the case, we may tend to feel rejected, dominated by 'heavy-handed' authority, or very fearful when a situation is really intended by God to help us grow. If we generally experience this, it may be that we have yet to learn fully how to grow in certain areas of our lives—especially as that relates to learning from disappointment. (If this is the case, it may be a good idea to read David Seamands' books, *Healing for Damaged Emotions* and *Putting Away Childish Things* [Victor Books].)

In the final analysis, dealing with disappointment, and responding to whatever God may be teaching us, will have more to do with how secure we feel in the Father's love, and how close we are to the Father's heart than anything else.

When Jesus knelt alone to talk to the Father, on that black night in the garden of Gethsemane, his heart was heavy. He faced death. He faced agony and unbelievable suffering. His Father had asked a hard thing of him. He was not forced to obey against his will. He obeyed the Father because he knew him and trusted him.

He said, 'Not my will, but thine, be done' (Lk 22:42), but that does not mean it was against his will. It was an honest statement of commitment to the will of the Father, in spite of what he felt about the certain suffering he faced.

The Father whom Jesus addressed in the garden, he knew to be great in patience and mercy, absolutely unending in love and kindness, and bountiful in provision and care. Because he knew the Father, he trusted him and obeyed him. It was not a forced response to an overbearing Father, but a trusting response to known love.

In this book I have written much of God's love and our response to his love. He does ask much of us, but he gives much. He is what one man called 'absolute demand and ultimate succour'. As Thomas Smail says in his book *The Forgotten Father* (page 37), '... the one in whom we call, is the God of Gethsemane who can ask for anything including ourselves, because he has given everything including himself'.

Healing and freedom from selfishness is God's ultimate desire for us. Try as we might, that will not happen through all the various means we can devise to improve ourselves, but only by returning to the one who created us, who longs for a relationship with us, who even now waits for us, and who indeed sent his Son to die for us.

EPILOGUE

I hold in my hand a newspaper clipping about junkie babies. These babies are born junkies. They were junkies before they came into the world—fed the drug while still in their mother's womb. They experience cold turkey as soon as they are born, shuddering and vomiting, and wracked with heroin withdrawal symptoms.

A special unit has been set up for these babies in the maternity section of Amsterdam's Academic Medical Centre. Though they are given loving care by the nurses and doctors, they are born into a living hell. Their mothers are junkies, most of them prostitutes.

I have seen what happens to them as they grow up. I live in a street in Amsterdam's Red Light district where some of them are brought up. To blot out the shame of giving birth to a child who suffers so much, some of the mothers take even more drugs. Sometimes the children are left in their rooms for hours while their mothers roam the streets 'working'. Men come and go, most are there for a few hours or days, or if the children are lucky they may have a father-figure even longer.

Why am I telling you about these pitiful junkie babies and their needy mothers? For two reasons. One is to remind you that there are many people in life who have it much worse than you. The second is to ask you to do something about it. Not just for the junkie babies, but also for those people around you who are in need. If we don't get involved in serving and caring for others in some way, we can become more and more ingrown. Our own problems will grow out of all perspective, and we can eventually become very selfish. Serving others is one way the Father provides for our own spiritual and emotional growth.

As already mentioned in this book, I have been called by God to serve him and others in the inner city of Amsterdam. Our family is part of a wonderful community of people who love God and who have found their fulfilment in life through serving him in this city.

We have found that the principles and truths described in this book really work. And we are learning more every day. Serving God is a wonderful adventure, especially when you are part of a missionary community—a family of brothers and sisters learning to make the Father's love a reality, both to one another and to those who do not know the Father.

We are also part of an international, interdenominational organization sharing the gospel in many different nations of the world. If you have been helped by this book and it has motivated you to want to help others, there are many opportunities for service. Of course your service to God and others should begin where you are, but if you are also interested in helping others in a place like Amsterdam, or London, or one of the other big cities in the world, for a summer, a year, or even longer, please visit ywam.org for information about opportunities for service. We also run three-month training programmes in counselling, biblical studies, basic discipleship, leadership training and cross-cultural missions. Young and old alike are welcome.

If you would like more information on how to get involved in any of these programmes in Amsterdam, please visit www.ywamamsterdam.com. YWAM is also involved in urban missions in the United Kingdom, and runs training programmes for those interested. For further information please visit www.ywamengland.org.

APPENDIX A

GUIDELINES FOR SELECTING A PSYCHIATRIST OR COUNSELLOR

Unfortunately it is possible that poorly skilled people can prey on sincere Christians by calling themselves counsellors. In addition, some psychiatrists can confuse or undermine the faith of Christians, in times of depression or need, by attacking their Christian faith.

A well-trained counsellor or psychiatrist can be a tremendous help to a Christian in need *if* they are sympathetic to their Christian faith. They are specialists just as doctors are often specialists. We should not expect them to fulfil the role of a spiritual leader, whose responsibility it is to provide spiritual help to the person in need, but they can be a great help in their area of speciality.

Here are some practical guidelines for choosing a counsellor or psychiatrist:

1. The best way to select a counsellor or psychiatrist is to rely on a referral from a respected church leader, family

doctor, or friend who has had previous contact with the professional and knows them and their work personally.

2. A competent professional is not threatened if a prospective patient calls and tactfully asks about their qualifications, their theoretical orientation, and the type of licence they hold.

3. Fees should be discussed before any commitment is made to treatment. A therapist should be willing to give at least a rough estimation as to how many sessions are going to be necessary, and at what intervals they will need to occur.

4. It is a good idea to find out how much experience the therapist has had in dealing with your particular problem. Some therapists are obviously better suited to certain areas.

5. Find out how much of the therapist's counselling is based on God's word. Does his counselling differ from that of a secular counsellor?

APPENDIX B

THE USE AND ABUSE OF AUTHORITY

Because of the tendency of good but sometimes immature leaders to respond to selfish or needy people with overbearing authority, and because of the influence of cult figures on so many unwary young people, it is important to be aware of some of the unhealthy extremes leaders can go to in exercising their leadership.

Hopefully the checklist below will not only help members of organizations or congregations evaluate the kind of authority they are following, but will also help sincere leaders do some 'soul-searching' if they are leading out of insecurity or are responding wrongly to those with needs in their group.

Included here are biblical principles for leaders to follow in responding to those people in their congregation or group that have need of loving confrontation. I have also included some guidelines on how to respond to leaders when they are wrong.

Extremism on the question of authority is easy to find: some go to one extreme and propound a kind of Christian anarchism where everyone is a law unto themselves with no need for accountability or submission; others go to the other extreme and teach a pyramid authority structure that undermines the priesthood of the believer and exalts authority figures to a place God never intended them to have. Those who dare to live in the 'radical middle' will no doubt make mistakes in finding their way, but will in the end enjoy the rewards of their efforts: deep friendships, godly accountability, the serenity of surrendering others to the Lord and the peace of living in a manner that is pleasing to our Father.

I am a bit uncomfortable with those who appoint themselves to be 'watchdogs' for the body of Christ, especially when they are quick to judge or are harsh in their spirit. Perhaps this is another form of authoritarianism. Obviously we need those who are called by God to serve the church by discerning the 'inroads of apostasy', but it is very important that they do their research thoroughly and without bias, and that they pray for those they find to be immature or unbiblical. Those who do this kind of research have an additional responsibility to be mature, discerning Christians (Jas 3:1). They need to seek out those they find to be in extremism and give them a chance to both explain themselves and repent if they have been wrong (Mt 5:21–26, 7:1–5; Gal 6:1–3). I have known of instances where those researching cults have judged others in the body of Christ wrongly and have hurt and damaged people to the same extent that they were accusing others of doing.

The following information contains principles that should, I believe, be applied equally to all those in the body of Christ.

1. Insistence on sharing all things in common

Insisting on giving up private ownership can be a way of controlling people's lives.

2. Treatment of women

When women are not given any authority, or are not recognized as equal to men through respect for their opinions, then authoritarianism is sure to follow.

3. The power of leaders

The Scripture teaches us to submit to those whom the Lord has placed over us (Acts 20:28–31; 1 Tim 1:3, 4:11; Tit 1:13; 3:1; Heb 13:17). The question is: how much and where? The Bible makes clear that in specific areas leaders do have authority, but there are very definite limits to this authority. For example, a leader does not have the right to tell people what to do in their personal lives. If you think through all the illustrations in the Scriptures where elders and apostles were exercising authority, can you think of any instance where any of the leaders, even in the crisis days of the early church in Jerusalem, ever tried to dominate or control somebody's life? Even Peter made the clear comment that Ananias and Sapphira could have kept all their money and property. Doing what everyone else was doing was not mandatory. The sin was not in what they kept, but in lying. There are no illustrations in the New Testament that are even remotely similar to the control being exercised by some elders or leaders over God's people today.

Leaders do not have the right to confirm people's personal guidance as to whether they get married, continue working in full-time Christian service or go to another place in that service. It is a privilege to pray with others about their personal guidance, but not a right. Obviously a leader can give a word of caution or counsel from the word for a person, but that should be shared as a friend. To confuse the two is to bring people under condemnation and make them feel obligated to do what the person is saying because he is an authority figure.

4. Turnover in leadership

If there is a rapid turnover in leadership every two or three years, it could be an indication that the leader is not the kind of person who can win long term friendships due to instability in his life or an overbearing personality. It is very important for those in an organization to ask how long those working closely together actually stay with their leader.

5. The leader's reaction under pressure

If the leader is consistently defensive, it may show that he is insecure, unsure of himself and his work. He may try to exercise a great deal of control over others and is often unsure of himself and may express his insecurity through authoritarianism.

6. Exclusiveness

Any time a group has an exclusive view towards its role in the church, it could be an indication not only of pride but of authoritarianism. Do they recognize all other committed Christians as believers and a part of the body of Christ? Beware of those who categorize some Christians as being more special to God, or having a revelation or experience or doctrine that produces the fruit of pride or exclusiveness.

7. The psychological make-up of a leader

Does the leader have in his nature a need to control others within his environment? There are some people who have this psychological flaw. The Lord can use this man, but he must have God break this in his life or he will tend towards authoritarianism and manipulation. Sometimes this trait surfaces in the beginning of a ministry, or it could come out later in a time of crisis or conflict.

8. Group conformity

There is always some need for conformity, particularly among organizations that have policies and procedures necessary for the accomplishing of their goals. However, these policies and goals should be open for the scrutiny of all in the body of Christ, and should be made with the counsel of godly people outside the organization. They should be explained to those who join the organization before any commitment of membership is made, so that the individuals understand what would be expected of them beforehand.

9. Leaving the group

When individuals want to leave the group, are they made to feel guilty, or is pressure put on them to stay? Do they feel hurt when they leave? Do they feel like they are second-class Christians if they are not staying with the group but going back to a local church? Would they feel comfortable in returning for a visit?

10. Possessiveness of staff and fellow workers

Does the leader make those who work with him feel obligated to stay? Is there a constant pressure used by the leadership to manipulate people into staying with the group? Do they feel somehow they have to break out in order to leave the group? Is 'guidance' or 'covering' used as a way of keeping people in the group? This kind of possessiveness can often lead to great hurts and make people feel very condemned for leaving.

11. Atmosphere of mistrust

Do the leaders use rules, regulations, scriptures and policies to control people's lives? Or do they create an atmosphere of grace and trust? Do the leaders rely upon people's maturity, or do they continually imply that the people cannot be trusted and 'laws' must exist to regulate people's behaviour? Obviously there must be a certain amount of submission, particularly in missionary organizations that have developed policies and procedures in order to be more efficient in achieving their goals. But even then those policies should be based on trust and not forced on those who disagree. Hopefully potential areas of disagreement will be discovered before a candidate joins a missionary society, but if not they should be given the freedom to leave (if conflict does arise) with appreciation for one another and a simple agreement that it is best for a parting of the ways.

12. Questions and criticisms

Can members of the group bring up their questions or make constructive criticism without the leadership becoming defensive? Are the leaders secure enough and mature enough in the Lord to encourage people to share hurts or disappointments, or ask questions about things they disagree with, without fear of recrimination or being judged as 'critical and rebellious'? Are the leaders accountable to somebody else besides themselves and 'the Lord'? Are they open to be corrected?

13. Overwork

Does the leadership make the members of the group feel obligated to work long hours, burning the candle at both ends? Some leaders drive their people and make them feel guilty for having personal time for hobbies, recreation, letter writing etc. Leaders can be guilty of burning their people out and placing them under condemnation for wanting the time necessary to be refuelled and refreshed in order to keep doing their work with the emotional strength that they need.

14. Moral impurity

Often those who become authoritarian or manipulative have compromised morally and are living in sin.

15. Role confusion: inspirational and pastoral leadership

A leader can become authoritarian or abusive in his leadership if he does not learn to distinguish the difference between personal counselling and visionary inspiration. It is one thing to stand in front of a group and inspire the group with 'the word of the Lord' for the direction of the group; it is quite another thing to be involved in personal counselling. If the leader approaches his pastoral counselling in the same style and manner as he would to inspire the whole group, he can come across as overbearing or overwhelming to those he is counselling. His role in counselling is to

remind people of scriptural principles and encourage them
to seek the Lord and to put God first in obeying his word.
It is not his responsibility to tell people what to do, or to
correct the errors in their life, but more to encourage them
to be open and obedient to the Lord.

16. Ownership of policies and major decisions

Do the leaders give the people an opportunity to feel
involved at a grass-roots level in decisions that are being
made in the group? Are decisions handed down arbitrarily
from the top without any opportunity for others to par-
ticipate in the decision? Do the people feel they can be a
part of shaping the policies of the community and not be
rebellious if they question them?

17. Over-emphasis on man's responsibility

Too much emphasis in this area without emphasizing God's
grace and mercy produces condemnation and doubt about
God's love and forgiveness. It is the loving kindness of God
that leads men to repentance.

18. Taking too much responsibility to correct problems in people's lives

People must be free to respond to the Lord when they are
ready to do so. Trying to be the Holy Spirit for people always
leads to conflict and hurt.

19. Denying people the right of appeal

If someone disagrees with a decision or is denied the right
to go to others for counsel when they disagree with a
leader, is to 'box' a person in. The leader is at the very least

exerting undue pressure on the person concerned, and may be revealing a basic insecurity and an unhealthy need to be in control.

20. Not admitting faults, or refusing to lead from a position of weakness

The leadership may make mistakes or somehow be a part of a situation that is unjust. This can include putting people under immature leadership and then blaming them for not co-operating; or exploiting their financial generosity. In such circumstances we should admit our failures and weaknesses and ask forgiveness from those who have been hurt. If a leader does not do that he will tend to blame others for their reactions and accuse them of 'having the wrong attitude' of 'being in rebellion'.

21. Teaching that a leader should always be obeyed no matter what he says because he is 'God's anointed'

Guidelines for church discipline

We should teach people to obey God and his word, not men. Obviously people need to deal with independence and an unbroken spirit, but that should be dealt with in the opposite spirit: gentleness and love. When there is a need for confrontation over bad attitudes, the following scriptural guidelines should be followed:

(1) Galatians 6:1–3 Go in a spirit of gentleness and humility, 'looking to ourselves lest we too be tempted'.

(2) Proverbs 18:17; Deuteronomy 17:2–7; 1 Timothy 5:19. Always hear both sides of a matter and

thoroughly look into all the points of view
before a judgement is made.

(3) James 3:13–18; 5:19–20; Matthew 18:15–18.
Follow the spirit of love outlined in these
passages. *Seek in every way to be redemptive. Never
put people in a position where it is hard for them
to return or seek counsel or find help from others.*
Remember that the portions of Scripture on
church discipline in Matthew are preceded and
followed by injunctions to 'not despise one of
these little ones' (speaking of a straying or lost
sheep) and to forgive our brother 'seventy times
seven'—which does not mean exactly four
hundred and ninety!

(4) 1 Samuel 12:23. Pray for those you are
concerned about, to make sure you have God's
heart for them and are not reacting to them
out of your own hurt or disappointment, even
the disappointment that comes out of love for
a person that you know could have done much
better. We must pray until we have God's heart
for a person, then go to them when we sense
God has prepared their heart for the correction.
Timing can be everything.

(5) Proverbs 11:14; 15:22; 24:6. When there is a
difficulty with someone's attitude, seek the
counsel of a mature, older pastor (particularly the
pastor of the person involved) on how to respond.
There is great protection and wisdom in seeking
the counsel of others, especially from older
more mature men outside one's own group or

organization. The willingness to seek this counsel shows a caution that reflects maturity and a real desire for what is best for the person involved.

In addition to the above mentioned principles it is important to point out that Christian organizations and missionary societies need the freedom to dismiss people if they do not co-operate with group policy, or if they develop a divisive or factious attitude. This is different from church discipline in that it has to do with maintaining the morale and unity of the group and being faithful to the vision and calling God has given the missionary society. Para-church organizations and missionary societies have the responsibility to spell out in writing their goals and policies *before* a person joins the group, so that they are not acting arbitrarily and the person understands what level of commitment is necessary in order to support its goals and policies. People must be told that involvement in the organization or appointment to the mission can be terminated if they are obviously a hindrance to fulfilling the goals of the organization. This should be done in a Christlike way and guidelines for how dismissals are handled should be written into the group's constitution, although this itself should include procedures for appeal to protect against abuse of authority.

How to respond to leaders when they are wrong

The principles above give us guidelines on how to respond to those that we are correcting when we are in a position of leadership or when we are going to a brother or sister in need. But what do we do when the leader over us, or any person in a position of authority, is wrong, either in their attitude or their actions? The following guidelines may be helpful:

(1) Make sure the facts are correct. Don't judge a person wrongly, and don't accept a charge against a person on the word of just one other person (Prov 18:17; Deut 13:12–15; 1 Tim 5:19). It is very important to hear all sides of a conflict before a judgement is made.

(2) Pray for the leader and make sure that you have no critical spirit or root of bitterness in your heart towards them. If you've been hurt or disappointed, make sure that you *keep on forgiving* until your heart is free of hurt. Make sure you maintain a heart of love, since love covers a multitude of sins (1 Pet 4:8). It is possible to lose objectivity about a situation through taking on the hurts of others. If you counsel with people who have been hurt by an authority figure and you take on their pain, you can take sides in the conflict and lose the opportunity both to offer sound biblical counsel to the one who is hurt (e.g. to forgive and pray for the ones who hurt them) and to be a minister of reconciliation and healing in the broken relationship.

(3) Pray for the leader that he will have a revelation from the Lord about the wrong that he's done or that he will know the right thing to do if he needs wisdom in the situation. It's extremely important that we intercede for him as an indication of our genuine commitment to the person and for God's best in the situation.

(4) If a leader has done something wrong and there is no change, seek God in humility if you are to speak to them. If it is an obvious wrong, such as stealing, being involved in a sexual sin, being dishonest etc, and you've gone to them and they do not repent, then go to another godly person in the body of Christ and ask them to go with you to talk to the person again (Mt 18:15–18; Lk 17:4).

(5) If there is no response and it is not a matter of serious disobedience to obvious moral principles, then do not go to others in the body of Christ criticizing the person concerned. The Bible does speak very strongly about the importance of unity and forgiveness in the body of Christ. To go to others when you disagree with a decision could put you in a position of causing a greater sin than the one you are concerned about in the life of the leader. There are strong warnings in the Scriptures about taking matters into our own hands and trying to correct them. Even David would not attack Saul in spite of his great sin, because God had put him in that position of leadership. David trusted God to bring an answer in the situation (1 Sam 24:6; see also Num 14; Eph 4:26, 29–32). If there is no response and it is a matter of moral wrongdoing, then take the matter to the leaders of the person's church, organization or denomination.

(6) If the leader is authoritarian or immature or very unwise, you have one of two options: you can stay under his authority and continue to

pray for him after you've gone to him to share your concern, or you can leave the group. It is important that you do not stay and become critical and bitter. You have the freedom before God to leave at any time that you feel the pressure is too great for you. But do not stay and become a source of division. If you do stay you should have the faith that God is going to bring a change in the situation and that he wants you there to be a blessing to others and for your own personal growth. God will vindicate you if you keep your heart right and continue to pray and believe the Lord. If it is a matter of moral impurity or compromise on orthodox doctrines such as the inspiration of the Scriptures, the divinity of Christ, the death and resurrection of the Lord Jesus, his atonement on the cross—then after bringing due notice to the person you should leave the group. To stay where there is moral impurity or doctrinal heresy could lead to compromise in your own life.

(7) *If you are unsure as to what to do,* seek counsel of godly people outside of the group. Go to a mature pastor or a leader in another organization, even if your leaders tell you not to do so! Every believer has that right.

At the same time that I point out some of the abuses of authority, it is important to affirm the great need for godly leaders. To become a wise leader means years of experience, which of course includes making mistakes and failing. The Scripture gives many examples of failure on the part of those who went on to be greatly used by God; this includes Moses, Abraham, Jacob, Joseph, David, Peter, Paul and many others.

There is a great need for wise fathers in the Lord who will take Timothies under their wings and encourage them and train them in godliness and wisdom. Where there is abuse of authority, obviously there needs to be correction, but *even more important there needs to be restoration and the kind of counsel and commitment that redeems one who has failed*. The leader who does that is indeed a rare and blessed person. May their kind greatly increase!

RECOMMENDED READING

Thomas A. Smail, *The Forgotten Father* (Hodder & Stoughton)

John Sanford, *Transformation of the Inner Man* (Bridge Publishing)

Ross Campbell, *How to Really Love Your Child* (Victor Books)

Gordon MacDonald, *The Effective Father* (Tyndale)

David Seamands, *Healing for Damaged Emotions* (Victor Books)

David Seamands, *Putting Away Childish Things* (Victor Books)

Charles Swindoll, *Dropping Your Guard* (Hodder & Stoughton)

Lawrence Crabb Jr, *Effective Biblical Counselling* (Zondervan)

Lawrence Crabb Jr, *Basic Principles of Biblical Counselling* (Zondervan)

Charles Paul Conn, *Father Care* (Word)